Charles Way

This collection of three plays is by one of Britain's leading writers of plays for children and young people. *'Red Red Shoes'* won the Arts Council's Award for Best Children's Play in 2004.

Charles Way was born in Devon in 1955, trained as an actor at the Rose Bruford College in London, then joined the Leeds Playhouse Theatre-in-Education team, for whom he wrote his first professional play in 1978. He became Resident Writer at Theatre Centre in London and has since written over forty plays including adaptations, radio, television and large-scale community theatre.

His work has been translated into French, German, Russian, Greek and Welsh and performed all over the world.

His play *'A Spell of Cold Weather'* (Aurora Metro) won the Writers' Guild Award for Best Children's Play in 1996. He was also invited to the Sundance Institute in Utah to work on *The Dove Maiden*, which subsequently toured Britain with Hijinx Theatre Co. Also published: *'The Classic Fairytales, retold for the stage'* (Aurora Metro)

He is a member of the Writers' Guild, and the Welsh Academy of Authors. He lives in Wales, with his wife and two children.

'...*more people in Wales have seen a Charles Way stage play than one by any other writer working here. He has also been produced in Britain more than any other living Welsh-based playwright... his plays can be complex, subtle, elusive, metaphorical, mythic, magical...*

David A----ms

aurora metro press

Founded in 1989 to publish and promote new writing, the press has specialised in new drama, fiction and work in translation, winning recognition and awards from the industry.

new drama

Theatre Centre, plays for young people, introduced by Rosamunde Hutt ISBN 0-9542330-5-0 £12.99

Young Blood, five plays for young performers
ed. Sally Goldsworthy ISBN 0-9515877-6-5 £10.95

Three Plays: Jonathan Moore
ISBN 0-9536757-2-6 £9.95

Best of the Fest. new plays celebrating 10 years of London New Play Festival ed. Phil Setren ISBN 0-9515877-8-1 £12.99

Black and Asian Plays Anthology introduced by Afia Nkrumah
ISBN 0-9536757-4-2 £9.95

Six plays by Black and Asian women writers
ed. Kadija George ISBN 0-9515877-2-2 £10.95

Seven plays by women, female voices, fighting lives
ed. Cheryl Robson ISBN 0-9515877-1-4 £5.95

Under Their Influence by Wayne Buchanan
ISBN 0-9536757-5-0 £6.99

Lysistrata – the sex strike after Aristophanes, adapted by Germaine Greer and Phil Willmott ISBN 0-9536757-0-X £7.99

Harvest by Manjula Padmanabhan
ISBN 0-9536757-7-7 £6.99

www.aurorametro.com

Charles Way

plays for young people

Introduced by the Author

Red Red Shoes

Eye of the Storm

Playing from the Heart

AURORA METRO PRESS

Contents

Foreword by Rosamunde Hutt   6

Introduction by Charles Way   9

Red Red Shoes   13
Introduced by Tony Graham

Eye of the Storm   67
Introduced by Gail McIntyre

Playing from the Heart   115
Introduced by Vicky Ireland

Plays produced and published   159

Foreword
Rosamunde Hutt

I have had the privilege of seeing Charles Way's plays from as many angles as you can imagine, having directed, co-produced and acted in his work over the years. I have sat in village halls from Abergavenny to Dorset with audiences helpless with laughter, and have watched children in schools and theatres spellbound as his particular form of magic unfolds. A friend once said of his work that you can spend an evening laughing aloud, then suddenly, without realising it, you are in the grip of something mythic – love has entered a loveless home, a child has been saved from a violent end, and you are unexpectedly, deeply moved.

Charles has written over forty plays, mainly for young people. I have followed his work ever since the early 1980's. His plays are regularly produced throughout Britain and on the international stage. In 1999, I saw a feast of his plays comprising three different Christmas shows in London at *Polka* Theatre For Children, the *Unicorn* Theatre For Children and the *Orange Tree* in Richmond. One of his specialities is engaging both adults and children in family shows, work that subverts the fairytale or the received opinion, that looks at the dark corners of life but comes laced with a sharp wit, warmth, poetry and humanity. His children's plays have led us through the looking glass, through tempests and tantrums, and into miniature and epic worlds, always encouraging the adult and the child to engage meaningfully and to acknowledge the magical in the everyday, as in *Eye of the Storm*.

Charles was the first writer I worked with as a director and I still abide by the rich nuggets that I learned from him – his insistence on working through metaphor, the discipline of plotting the differences between a narrative epic and a psychological journey, and where the twain shall meet, the need in us to explore the archetype. He is always very clear about the impetus of a play and how that impetus, or wellspring, should inform the writing of every scene, every encounter.

I have witnessed the sweep of his preoccupations, as he has created a body of socially and politically engaged work but I've also noticed how he returns repeatedly to certain key themes: love, the complexities of human nature, and the importance of storytelling, often bearing witness to events on the world's stage and to collective and individual acts of courage. Some of his characters rage against their circumstances, for example, Betty in *A Spell of Cold Weather*. Others take action, determined to take charge and make a difference, as exemplified by Evelyn in *Playing from the Heart*.

I think it significant that Charles has dedicated so much of his work to theatre outside of the mainstream. He has stated that, 'The act of theatre is an act of society and an act of hope'. I think it crucial to an examination of his work that often a Charles Way play will be a child or young person's first introduction to the power of theatre, a moment that might kick start a life-long relationship with the art form. His work introduces theatre as part of everyday living – the shared experience in the nursery, the church hall, the community centre. Significant too, is the fact that he has nurtured longstanding collaborative partnerships with many companies and artists: Gwent Theatre in Education Company, Theatre Centre, the Unicorn, Polka, New Perspectives, Hijinx Theatre, the Sherman Theatre Company, developing plays sometimes through improvisation with actors, prioritising the use of music and of dance. Here is a playwright who believes in the power of the community.

At the heart of his success with children's plays is, I think, a very special truth. It is not just that his plays are child-centred, speaking to the children in the audience with direct simplicity, but that the child in his work often transforms something that is undernourished, that needs to flower. In a world where children are often powerless, neglected or marginalised, audiences recognise that he sees the child as a catalyst for change, as in *Red Red Shoes*.

Back to Dorset in 1993, at a packed performance of *In the Bleak Midwinter*, a show for families, where an audience member joyfully quoted the following line to me afterwards. Miriam the realist says critically to Zak her husband, 'An' to pass the time you 'ave to find meaning an' honour in humble things.' What Miriam, the character, saw as a frustrating habit, the audience member saw as summing up the spirit of the play and the evening. Zak the dreamer, insists that, 'Life is full of meaning, as the sky is full of stars.' Charles searches for meaning in a world that to both the adult and the child can appear confusing, meaningless, impoverished. He finds meaning in humble things and therefore makes the ordinary, heroic. Because of this, I am convinced his work will endure: it is contemporary and timeless, charged in recent years by country rhythms, the seasons, a sense of wonder and the cycle of life. Always commenting on our times, unafraid to tackle spiritual, moral and political matters, he looks at the stuff of life, tenderly, compassionately and with a sense of humour.

Rosamunde Hutt is the Director of Theatre Centre, and has worked extensively in Theatre for Young People throughout Britain, specialising in collaborating with writers on original plays.

Introduction
Charles Way

I have often wondered what it is that makes an author write for children. Lewis Carroll wrote brilliantly about the central predicaments of childhood; feeling small, lost, in a strange unreasonable world. Carroll was expressing something that we feel, not only as children but all our lives, and this is why his work endures. For my part I write plays that seem to be about the journey of childhood and the three plays in this book all involve children/young people and their relationship with the adult world and their progression into it. This journey into a new state of self-knowledge is a metaphor for the whole of life's journey. I would like to think therefore, that my plays, while entirely suitable for young people are not exclusively for them; plays that bring widely different age groups together, and give a common experience. This seems to be one of the most important aspects of modern theatre, existing as it does in a world which divides us into not so neat groups – pre-school, infant, junior, teenage, young adult, young married with two incomes, etcetera until death us do depart. Of course some plays are not suitable for young people and this is not to do with theme, but rather subject matter and the treatment of it. By themes I mean, forgiveness, grief, love, change, hope, despair, evil, and so forth. These themes and many more will be found in the plays in this book.

Eye of the Storm is based on *The Tempest*, reputedly Shakespeare's last play and a mature reflection on mortality, power, change and forgiveness. *Eye of the Storm*, takes the same themes but looks at them through the other end of time's telescope. It is Miranda's story.

When I first wrote the script, it was to provoke debate among young people about gender roles. I hope that it still does, but when I rewrote the play for the West Yorkshire Playhouse ten years later, I had teenage children of my own and was rather more sympathetic to Prospero, the well-meaning dad. The result is a new play that dramatises the struggle for freedom and the gains and losses that come with it. From Miranda's point of view, she gains responsibility over her own life, but loses the protection of her father's island. She must face the reality of her father's future death, and thus at some far distant time, her own. Prospero, for his part, must face up to his own life. Has he been a good father? A good husband? Has he been a kind master and can he let go of the power he has worked so diligently to maintain? These questions and many others tumble out in a comic caper involving mistaken identities and cross-dressing. Essentially, *Eye of the Storm* is about seeing the other person's point of view – something that isn't easy at any age.

In its various incarnations, *Eye of the Storm*, has been a treat to watch because the designers have enjoyed creating the strange world of Prospero's kingdom. In its most recent production, spectacular puppets were used to help tell the story and to act as a metaphor about control. Costume has invariably involved a mix of modern and Shakespearean dress, a mix which is reflected in the blend of poetry and vernacular speech that pushes the play along. It is, even in the small scale, an attempt at total theatre involving text, movement spectacle and sound.

This notion of total theatre is pushed further in *Playing from the Heart*. It tells the story of how the young Evelyn Glennie persevered, despite profound deafness to become a professional musician. Story however, is not the only factor here. The text is a platform from which to explore a journey through sound and movement. The play was written for a small professional cast plus a single percussionist, but interestingly, it's currently being performed in New Zealand with a cast of young people and a full orchestra.

Some reviews have described *Playing from the Heart* incorrectly, as an adaptation of Evelyn Glennie's autobiography. This is not the case, although the book was very useful. The subject of the play was suggested to me by Vicky Ireland, the director of the Polka Theatre and it took me some time to come round to the whole idea mainly because I wasn't that sure what I, a hearing writer, could say or explore. When I met Evelyn, and saw her perform, I realised however, that she is a kind of living metaphor for all of us who have ever been told as children or as adults, that we should accept someone else's reality, even if it means the squashing of our hopes. Evelyn Glennie's experience is important because her success and her musicianship challenge our notion of reality, and this is part of, if not the whole function of art.

Where *Playing from the Heart* has sound as its centre, *Red Red Shoes* has dance. *Red Red Shoes* progresses, I hope, further still into 'total theatre' and is the most experimental of the three plays in this book. It was a very difficult play to write, but one, which I felt was waiting inside me to be written. It's difficult because it approaches the opposite side of the coin in terms of childhood experience to the one shown in *Playing from the Heart*.

Writing this introduction has confronted me with the question of why I wrote this story. I think it's because what happens to children has become part of the way in which we judge our society, and how we decide what's right or wrong. Several high profile cases, such as the killing of Jamie Bulger, the release of his killers, and the death of Damilolah Taylor have provoked intense debate about what makes moral beings. On March the third 1999, *The Guardian* published a picture of a mother and child at a border camp just outside of Kosova. The child is trying to comfort a grief-stricken adult. This isn't what we expect; it's all in reverse, but it raises the question in me about childhood morality. Children are not fully formed moral beings and very occasionally they do something entirely wrong. *Red Red Shoes* explores the reverse notion that a child could, even in the face of adult mayhem and war, perform an act that shocks because it is so 'right' and rebalances the world.

I would like to thank all those who have been part of the creation of these plays, particularly those who have commissioned and developed them through workshops, toward final production. These plays have come into existence against the tide, as it were. Children's theatre writing is rarely reviewed and if it is, it's not easy for the reviewer to persuade the editor of its importance or relevance to our cultural life. Children's theatre has changed over the past ten years. It is no longer either just educational, or just entertainment. The two worlds of Theatre in Education, and Children's theatre have in some ways fused and very fine plays for children, capable of winning any writing award are now being produced. The Arts Council of England has recently created a Children's Playwriting Award and this is an important step forward, [not least because it actually involves money]. It shows that children's theatre is a serious business, a serious art form that has to be nurtured, not for its own sake but for the children who see the work. Their need for stories which empower them and show that change is possible, is as pertinent today as ever. Perhaps this is why I continue to write for children, although I suspect the danger of children's audiences is also an attraction, since they have very clear ways of expressing boredom or dissatifaction. The opposite is also true. Recently a ten year old child, who lives in our street, asked when my next play would be on and when I told her she clenched both fists in front of her face and cried out, 'I can't wait, I just can't wait!' She made my day.

Red Red Shoes

Red Red Shoes

Charles Way is a playwright not only highly skilled at his craft but also prepared to take risks. His plays for children, like the rest of his work, contain much that is complex, poetic and profound. Children's theatre rarely scales the heights achieved by much contemporary children's literature. In *Red Red Shoes* he has written a play that, in its soul-searching honesty, will capture children's attention like few plays do.

Inspired by Powell and Pressburger's iconic film, I suggested to Charles that he write a version of *The Red Shoes* for older children that would contain within it, space for contemporary dance. What came back was quite unexpected. Although unidentified by name, it is set in the war zone of former Yugoslavia.

Franvera, the young girl at the heart of this new play, has a powerful dream to be a dancer. Single-mindedly pursuing her dream, she barely sees the war clouds gathering around her. Forced to flee from her village, Franvera is poised between life and death. As the play unfolds though, it appears that she is not in her home village with her family, on the march with Red Beard and other refugees, fleeing through a forest, climbing a mountain to reach the border – she is, instead, in a room without walls. Her traumatic tale is finding its voice, its shape, its stark imagery with the aid of a *doctor* – maybe a therapist?

The dominant image of *Red Red Shoes* is, like much of the play, borrowed from Hans Christian Andersen's strange, dark tale. A girl is given a new pair of red shoes, puts them on and finds that she cannot stop dancing. That is her sin as well as her redemption. In his new version, Charles has placed this haunting image in a context where a cycle of nationalist revenge is a much more deadly sin. Yet, the play does not reach out for simple, obvious truths. It thrives on the ambiguity of the original metaphor. For one all too brief moment, the world stops what it is doing to look at Franvera, as she dances a furious dance, born of hope and renewal. The dance of death and the dance of life are counterpoised beautifully in this exquisite and painfully moving new play for children.

Tony Graham, Unicorn Theatre for Children

Red Red Shoes

Inspired by Hans Christian Andersen's 'The Red Shoes'.

The play was jointly commissioned and first performed in September 2001 by Unicorn Theatre for Children and The Place, London. Directed by Tony Graham, choreography by Dan O'Neill, music by John Avery, design by Russell Craig and lighting by Jeanine Davies.

CHARACTERS	CAST
Franvera	Christine Devaney
Mother	Emily Piercy
Father	Tom Yang
Anna	Dawn Hudson
Old Lady	Mary McCusker
Red Beard	Simon Thomson
Doctor	Tom Yang

The cast takes on various roles as villagers, guests, children at the border, soldiers etc.

<u>*Notes:*</u>

The play takes place in a country like Britain, or any modern nation, which accepts refugees. The action for the most part takes place in a room, in a medical establishment. It would be truer to say, however that the play takes place in the head of a traumatised child. The set design should reflect this reality above any other.

It was originally conceived as dance theatre for a cast of six or seven but could be performed by a much larger group, as it is the people of Franvera's village as 'Cast' who tell the story. Much of the text given to the 'Cast' can be acted or danced, rather than spoken.

CAST   Once upon another country
so very near, so very far away
there lived a girl.
happy and hopeful
she ran to school,

but home she flew
like a bird, or an angel.
Yes, just like an angel.
It was as if, her feet were wings
and could not touch the ground.

MOTHER   Here comes Franvera.

FATHER   Hey – stop, stop – did you hand in your maths
homework?

FRANVERA Yes.

FATHER   Good. I'd like to know how I did.

FRANVERA Where are you going?

CAST   He does not answer but blows a whistle at her,
the one he uses for football.
The one he wears round his neck
like a lucky charm.

MOTHER   He won't be long. Now run down to the shop and
buy some bread from the old lady. We have people coming
tomorrow.

FRANVERA Tomorrow? What's tomorrow?

MOTHER   Yes, yes. Go, as fast as your legs can carry you.

CAST   There she goes dancing down the village street.
She never stops moving.
Sometimes she dances when she brushes her teeth.
Sometimes she dances when she helps her mother
hang out the weekly wash,
and some would smile and say–
There goes Franvera.
One day she'll take off
and land in another country.
But some would scowl and say–
Look at that girl, always on the move
doesn't she know these are dark days
and there she is dancing without a care in the world.
Oh but she had cares enough.

Cares that hung heavy on her shoulders like a wet coat.

Why was she in trouble with the Maths teacher?

Why was her hair so straight?

Why did her thoughts run like mountain goats
through the night and stop her sleeping?

Why were her parents whispering the other night
behind a closed door?

Why does her best friend stop her in the street this very day

and say –

ANNA Franvera?

FRANVERA Anna! What's the matter, what's happened?

ANNA My father says, I can no longer play at your house.

FRANVERA Why does he say that?

ANNA He says there's trouble coming. Everyone's talking about it. Haven't your parents talked about it?

FRANVERA Yes, all the time, but they said we should stay friends. They said for you to come over…

ANNA I can't. I can't. Not anymore.

FRANVERA Why not?

ANNA Last night at supper, I said you were my best friend… father slapped my face, in front of everyone. He said from now on, I can only speak to my own people. If I see you on the street I have to walk on the other side. If I don't, he will be angry, like a storm. I can't speak to you. Never.

FRANVERA Never?

ANNA Why don't you just go – leave? This is not your country – that's what he said.

FRANVERA If you won't speak to me, then I won't speak to you.

ANNA Franvera?

FRANVERA I hate you – I hate you.

CAST Franvera can hardly believe her own lips.

Her friend is running away and there's no time
to take the words back.

OLD LADY   Franvera?

FRANVERA   Yes?

OLD LADY   I've never seen you standing so still before. Like a post in the ground.

FRANVERA   My mother would like the bread she ordered.

OLD LADY   Yes, yes. There's no need to rush.

I used to rush when I was young.

Where did it get me? Nowhere.

I'm still living in the same village.

FRANVERA   Always – the same village?

OLD LADY   Oh yes– those were dark days,

the days of my childhood.

One day I will tell you – but not now.

FRANVERA   Thanks for the bread.

OLD LADY   It's not free you know. Good.

I will see you again tomorrow.

FRANVERA   Tomorrow?

CAST   For the first time in a long time

Franvera does not run home.

CAST   The next day at two o'clock in the afternoon,

the sun warm with the promise of summer

many relatives came.

Old men with blue rough cheeks and bright neckerchiefs

bring guitars and violins.

They play all through a lunch of bread, soup and spicy sausage.

And their round wives in black headscarves

nod their heads and tap their toes

in tight black shoes.

Franvera dances between them with trays of food

and aunties and uncles smile and ask–

CAST   What are you dreaming of, hey Franvera?

CAST   Will you stay in the village?

	So many leave, these days.
CAST	The young should stay and make this country strong.
CAST	If they leave what happens to our language?
CAST	What happens to our land?
CAST	Shush! It's rude to talk of such things at a party.
CAST	What are you going to be Franvera, hey? What are you going to be tomorrow?
CAST	When you grow a little taller?
FRANVERA	Tomorrow? What's tomorrow?
CAST	When the eating's done

the musicians begin to play
a song Franvera knows.
She turns and sees her father
take her mother by the hand
and slowly begin to dance.
"Oh beauty, O beauty when I saw your eye
that day when you were passing by,
two or three words I said to you.
Come here, come here to my soul
Because without you my life will be empty forever.
Two or three sweet words for the burning heart.
Together with everything else, I gave you my love."
Her mother dances like a gypsy
her hands slowly curving in the air
as if she could spin heavenly cloth
out of nothing.

Franvera sees that her mother is a little vain
and her father, a little proud, his head held high and
rather stiff
and her love for them goes straight from her heart to
her feet
making her toes itch inside her school shoes.

	Then there is loud applause
	and they laugh and step back
	as if it was nothing.
MOTHER	Please now will everyone be quiet for a moment.
CAST	But some of the men have had too much to drink.
MOTHER	Be quiet please – we have a present for Franvera.
CAST	Her father takes her by the hand and leads her forward,
	and the old sausage smelling ladies grin without teeth ,
	cluck their tongues and pat her head.
FATHER	Twenty years ago we were married.
	For ten years we dreamt of a child.
CAST	You were doing it the wrong way.
CAST	The old ladies slap their legs and laugh like hens
	and mother looks at Franvera as if to say–
MOTHER	One day the old ones will grow up.
FATHER	And when we had
	almost given up hope
	the dream came true.
CAST	Now her father is holding a box
MOTHER	I thought I told you to wrap it up.
CAST	Father does not like to be told off
	in front of his guests
	but today he cannot be angry
	so he shrugs–
FATHER	You know what kids are like
	you give them an expensive present
	and they play with the box.
	So this time I thought,
	Okay. I'll just give her a box.
CAST	The guests all laugh
	as Franvera's mother
	scolds her husband

with her dark eyes.

All this time Franvera is holding the box
and it feels so light,
like it must float away
if she lets go.

FATHER   Open the box Franvera.

CAST   She opens the box
and for the second time that day time is polite
and stops its going on and on,
as out of the box Franvera lifts
a pair of red shoes.

She's aware of the silence
that greets this pair of red red shoes.
No one here wears red ,
brown shoes, black shoes
but never red–
red is not a modest colour.

MOTHER   These are not ordinary shoes –

CAST   Explains her Mother to the old guests
in brown shoes, black shoes.
These are dancing shoes.

FATHER   Franvera is going to be a dancer.

MOTHER   She will dance in the city ballet.

CAST   Now they understand.

CAST   Dancing shoes–
Of course.

CAST   And lovely too, so soft.

CAST   But Franvera does not hear them approve or
              disapprove
              all she can hear is music, that begins slowly,
              like a wheel being pushed up hill.
              It reaches the summit then it rolls
              faster and faster, until she can hardly keep up.
              So her parents join hands
              and they dance,
              three in a ring
              as if no one else existed

ANNA   Franvera?
    Last night at supper, I said you were my best friend, and father
    slapped my face, in front of everyone. He said from now on, I can
    only speak to my own people. If I see you on the street I have to
    walk on the other side. If I don't, he will be angry, like a storm. I
    can't speak to you. Never.

FRANVERA   Never?

ANNA   Why don't you just go – leave? This is not your
    country – that's what he said.

FRANVERA   If you won't speak to me, then I won't speak to you.

ANNA   Franvera?

FRANVERA   I hate you – I hate you.

CAST   Now there is a room, and in the room
              sits a girl like Franvera.
              She looks so very like her
              but different, strange, tired, so tired.
              It's a strange room without walls
              just a bed and somewhere, far away
              she can hear voices, echoes, whispers.

              A ray of sun shines into the room
              and the girl who has been sitting on the bed
              staring at nothing in particular,

gets down and walks towards it.
She lets it fall on her face.
Yes it is Franvera, but she doesn't smile,
it's as if the sun were cold.
She closes her eyes and lets the sun
light up her pale cheeks.
The whispers fade and in her head
she hears faint traces of a gypsy tune,
but as the sun fades, so does the music.
She looks down at her feet
and sees that they are bare.
Bare feet, bare feet.
The thought seems to panic her
and she tries to leap free
of any contact with the earth
but every time she leaps, she lands,
and her feet become barer
until at last she runs back to her bed.

Now a man comes into the room.
He doesn't even knock.
She closes her eyes and pretends to sleep.

She hears him leave the room
but then he's back. She waits.
When she feels that he's gone
she turns, and sees some paper on the floor
and a stack of bright pens.

Why didn't he knock?
What right has he to come walking in
as if he owned the place?
She picks up a piece of paper
so new, so crisp.

She listens to the sound it makes
as one piece becomes two, three, four.
Soon she is surrounded by paper
and it looks just like her room
the night her maths refused to make itself simple.

Now she hears a new sound, heavy, grumbling,
like an engine, a tractor or a tank.
A tank?
Bare foot she runs across the room
her feet on fire
stares out of a naked window.
What does she see?
Something that makes her run and hide
throwing herself under the bed.

Franvera is under the bed
as the soldier comes into the room.
He stands by the bed
She stares at his boots,
so black so polished.
Where is mother, where is father?
What's happening?
The soldier sits on the bed
and lights a cigarette.
She looks at the back of his boots
so big, so black, so polished.

Then she draws a breath.
The doctor – is he a doctor?
comes in humming a tune
He can't see Franvera
because she's under the bed.
Franvera dare not move

because the soldier is there.
Why can't the doctor see the soldier?
Why doesn't he do something?
the doctor is looking now at Franvera.
Can he see her? Yes.

DOCTOR   Hello Franvera.

CAST   Franvera points at the soldier's boots.

DOCTOR   What is it?
What do you see?

CAST   Franvera does not speak,
she cannot speak.

She watches the soldier's boots walk
across the floor.
She cannot see the soldier
she can only see the boots
and these boots are joined now
by another pair, and now
everywhere she looks
there are black boots.

DOCTOR   Tell me what you see?

CAST   She covers her eyes and waits
and waits, and when she opens them
the boots have gone to the edges
of the edgeless room.

The doctor puts out his hand.
Perhaps she should bite it hard?
But no, what has he done? Nothing.
Slowly she crawls out, mouse from a hole.
She searches the room, looking for bootprints,
but doesn't find any, only some torn pieces of paper.

DOCTOR	It doesn't matter. It's only paper.
	Here, I've brought you something else.
	It's a map of your country.
	Perhaps you can show me
	the place you were born?
	A village? A town?
CAST	He puts the map on the floor
	and she looks down at it.
	How small her country seems,
	how far away.
DOCTOR	It's all rivers and mountains.
CAST	She runs her hand over the map
	as if she might feel the rocks on her skin,
	But it just feels flat.
	Its nothing , just a map.
DOCTOR	We can look at it again. Another time.
CAST	Yes, yes, another time.
	She sits on the bed and feels that it's wet.
DOCTOR	What? Oh. It doesn't matter.
CAST	But it does matter.
	Of course it matters.
	Why does he keep saying it doesn't matter?
	She rips off the sheets
	and throws them on the floor.
DOCTOR	They can be washed. It's easy.
CAST	He goes to pick them up
	but she grabs one end and pulls it hard
	then she throws it down again.
	He picks it up.
	She throws it down.
	He picks it up she throws it down.
	Now they have hold of an end each

and she is glaring at him.
Never has she been so angry.
If only she could make him disappear
but he won't, he's stubborn,
he just stands there like a fool.

DOCTOR   Franvera, your name is all I have.
Can you tell me other things?

CAST   The doctor is speaking, his lips are moving,
but Franvera doesn't hear him anymore.
she can't hear because now she's staring at the white sheet
as if seeing one for the first time.
And a breath of wind
passes right through her
and standing where the doctor stood just a moment ago
is her Mother, holding the sheet.

MOTHER   Are you going to help me or not?

CAST   Then she walks across the edge less room
like she was strolling across the back yard at home.
Is it a ghost? No – it really is her.

She hangs up the sheets to dry
singing to herself
but then she stops, looks to the sky.

A single beam of sun
burns a hole in the cloud
and lands in the backyard.

Franvera lifts up her face.

FRANVERA   Too much sunshine is bad for the skin.

MOTHER   Who told you that?

FRANVERA   A friend I used to have.

MOTHER	I'm sorry Franvera, about your friend.
	One day you can be friends again.
	It's going to rain before noon.
CAST	And as she says this
	the sun goes in behind a cloud
	and far off there is a roll of thunder.
FRANVERA	Thunder?
MOTHER	No.
FRANVERA	A cloud can be so many things.
MOTHER	Shh – listen.
FRANVERA	First it's a horse, then a cat,
	or an ice cream.
MOTHER	I can hear something.
FRANVERA	A car?
MOTHER	No. A truck or…
FRANVERA	A storm?
CAST	Now the sound is getting louder.
	Just like a heavy truck.
MOTHER	Go inside the house.
FRANVERA	But I want to see.
MOTHER	Go inside.
FRANVERA	It came from over there.
MOTHER	Wait here, don't leave the house till I get back.
FRANVERA	Where are you going?
MOTHER	I'll see who's coming.
	Do as you're told.
CAST	Franvera stands in the yard.
	Everything is the same as yesterday.
	Everything is the same.
	It was on this very spot her parents danced.
ANNA	Franvera.
FRANVERA	I thought you weren't speaking to me.
ANNA	Please listen.
FRANVERA	No, not anymore. Go away.

ANNA   But you have to listen – you have to. Last night soldiers came to see my father. They said, they'll come to the village and send away everyone who wasn't born here. He gave them names...

FRANVERA   I was born here.

ANNA   Your parents were not born here. They were born across the border and now they must go back.

FRANVERA   Go back? I don't understand. I'm not going anywhere.

ANNA   But you must go Franvera. You must go now. This country is not your country. I heard them say so.

FRANVERA   Anna?

CAST   Then there is thunder
and Franvera runs to her room
and hides under her bed.
She listens, no it's not thunder
It's bombs – falling near the village.
She covers her face. Silence.
When she opens her eyes
she is staring at the black boots
and the soldier is sitting on her bed
smoking a cigarette.
She dares not breathe
but somehow he knows she is there.
Now she is dragged out by her hair
like a dog from a kennel
who has done something terrible
but she has done nothing.

SOLDIER   Where's your father?

FRANVERA   He's at school.

SOLDIER   What does he do there?

FRANVERA   He teaches football.

SOLDIER   No. He does not teach football anymore.
Do you smell something – something burning?
Yes? That's the smell of the school turning to ashes.

	Your father wasn't there to stop us.
	Maybe he's gone up into the hills to clean his gun.
FRANVERA	He hasn't got a gun.
SOLDIER	You see – that's the trouble with you people,
	you don't even know your own parents.
	You think your father is teaching football,
	but all the time he is teaching something else.
	We know. We know.
CAST	Now he's looking round the bedroom.
	Beneath his feet, torn paper,
	and for a crazy moment
	Franvera wishes she had tidied up.
	But where is mother?
SOLDIER	What are these?
FRANVERA	My shoes
SOLDIER	Red shoes? What for?
FRANVERA	I'm going to be a dancer.
SOLDIER	Who says?
FRANVERA	Everyone.
SOLDIER	What do they say?
FRANVERA	They say I'm going to dance for my country.
SOLDIER	Put them on. Put on the red shoes.
	I'm a dancer too. Yes. And when I find your father
	I am going to dance on his grave.
	But first it's your turn. Show me.
	Dance. Dance!
FRANVERA	I can't.
SOLDIER	Why? Are you scared?
FRANVERA	I have no music.
SOLDIER	Music? You want music too?
	How spoilt you people are
	you want everything – the house
	the village – the fields – the mountains.
	You want the whole place for yourself.

	Well, you can't have it.
	But music? Of course.
CAST	The soldier begins to stamp his big boots
	on the bedroom floor.
SOLDIER	Now dance.
CAST	So Franvera begins to dance
	the steps she learnt at school.
	The steps she danced at her audition
	for the dancing school
	in the big city far away
	where one day she would dance for her country.
	Now the soldier is watching her
	his eyes moist with the beauty
	of the dancing girl in the red shoes.
SOLDIER	Stop. Stop!
	This house – this room –is not yours.
	Go away, and never come back.
CAST	The soldier has gone.
	Her Mother has gone.
	The soldier has gone.
	Her mother has gone...
	but the doctor returns pushing a trolley
	on which there is a computer.
DOCTOR	This is a computer.
CAST	She glares at him.
DOCTOR	Of course, you know what it is.
CAST	She sits on her bed and stares at the doctor.
DOCTOR	I see you're wearing your red shoes again.
	Why's that, Franvera?
CAST	She cannot answer.
	She is frozen, even her toes.
DOCTOR	You had a computer once?

You had one at school or home?
Perhaps you had one like this in your bedroom?
On this site are 74,000 names.
People like you, from many countries
People who have lost someone.
People who are lost, like you.

This is what you do.
You type in your own name.
F-R-A-N-V-E-R-A. Like so.

CAST Her toes melt.
Franvera walks to the screen
and sees her own name.

DOCTOR Have I spelt it correctly?
You need to type in your family name.
The name of your town, or village.
Then you type in the name of the person you wish to find.
You need these names.

CAST Franvera sits, types out her family name.

DOCTOR Good – It's a strong name.
Now type out the name of the person you wish to find.
Your mother perhaps?
You need her name.

CAST The doctor is speaking, his lips are moving,
but Franvera doesn't hear him anymore.
He's drifting away – soon he will be out of sight.
All she can see now is her mother
coming back into the room
her face swollen, her lip bleeding.

MOTHER What's happened? Are you alright?
FRANVERA Your face.
MOTHER Take off the red shoes.

FRANVERA   No –

MOTHER   You must, we're leaving. We have to go. We have two hours.

FRANVERA   I'm not leaving.

MOTHER   In two hours they'll burn the village. Be brave, please, for me. For me. You'll need good walking shoes and warm clothes.

FRANVERA   Where are we going?

MOTHER   Into the mountains, away from the soldiers.

CAST   Outside in the fields there's another explosion.

her bedroom shakes as if it too were afraid.

FRANVERA   What's happening?

MOTHER   They're shelling the fields to make us leave – so we leave.

FRANVERA   What about father?

MOTHER   He's coming – I phoned him.

CAST   Franvera starts to pack her school bag.

She empties her books on the floor.

What does one take?

She can't decide.

FRANVERA   You said this wouldn't happen. You promised.

MOTHER   Put this ring in your bag.

FRANVERA   Why?

MOTHER   Just do as you're told!

CAST   Gloves, scarves, socks.

She slips off the red shoes

is putting them in her bag.

MOTHER   Don't take them.

FRANVERA   But you gave them to me.

MOTHER   Don't take them!

CAST   She puts them to one side

and when her mother isn't looking

she puts them in her bag.

Now they are outside

and the village is new to her.
Smoke fills the air.
Soldiers wearing black boots
go in and out of houses shouting,
sometimes they come out carrying TV sets.
So many black boots,
and everyone she knows is outside
forming a long line leading away from the village.

The old lady who sells bread,
the dinner ladies from school.
There are no men.
Where are the men?
Where is father?

The soldier who made her dance
is stopping each person and taking things away;
papers, earrings, necklaces.

SOLDIER   Gold... Gold... give me your gold.
You people like gold – yes?

CAST   Now an old man is limping along behind them
and mumbling to himself , like a fool.
A soldier sees a young boy in the line
He goes to the same school –

SOLDIER   How old are you?

CAST   Sixteen.

SOLDIER   Take him to the schoolyard – take him.
Old ones – women – children .Go Go Go.

CAST   Suddenly he rips the bag from Franvera's back.
He empties it out.
He sees the red shoes
and throws them aside.
then he sees the ring
and grins like a schoolboy.

SOLDIER	Go Go Go
CAST	Franvera picks up her things
	and sees the old man is holding her red shoes.
	She takes them – and sees his hands
	looks up to his face.
	and it's her father
	pretending to be lame and stupid.
	He's wearing an old coat,
	covered in muck –
FRANVERA	Father?
MOTHER	Say nothing – nothing.
CAST	Now they are approaching the soldier
	who made Franvera dance.
	When he sees her, he smiles like they were old friends
	but then he stops smiling and stares at the fool behind.
SOLDIER	Who is this man?
	Who knows this man?
	I thought you people
	knew each other?
MOTHER	He's an idiot,
	his brain has gone.
SOLDIER	Hey Red Shoes
	who is this man?
MOTHER	I told you this man is an imbecile.
	He is nothing, he can't even speak.
SOLDIER	Go Go!
CAST	He yells in her face
	pushes her aside.
	Franvera dare not speak.
	Her mother stares at her
	her eyes are saying something.
SOLDIER	Who is he? Who is he?

FRANVERA	I don't know.
SOLDIER	You don't know the village fool?
	Strange, you who were born here?
CAST	Now the soldier takes his gun –
MOTHER	We don't know him.
CAST	And puts it to her father's head.
FRANVERA	Father!
CAST	She did not mean to say it.
	It just fell out of her.
SOLDIER	Well done Red Shoes!
FATHER	It's alright Franvera – it's alright.
CAST	His eyes fix on hers
	and there are years in them
	of love and worry
	of books read together
	of scoldings and sweets under pillows.
	Countless, nameless moments.
	And there is one moment more.
	He has taken the whistle from his neck
	and pressed it into her hands.
	She stares down at it and
	only faintly does she hear her mother's cries
	as her father falls under blows
	and is gone.
FRANVERA	Father! Father?
CAST	When she wakes it's still dark
	but she is no longer in the room.
	She is back in the forest
	with the sound of the forest
	and the big cold sky
	that never ends high above her.

All around her are people from the village
sitting, lying on the forest floor
and some are moaning softly
and it becomes a strange lament,
a sound of sorrow she's never heard before.

RED BEARD Be quiet. Do you want the soldiers
to hear you and come looking?

CAST The man who speaks is an old soldier
with a long woollen coat full of holes,
as if he had been shot a hundred times
but never killed.
He has a beard that is so red
it glows in the darkness.

All day they had walked
higher and higher into the hills
into the land of the eagle.
They walked until their precious belongings
became too heavy and were left behind,
they walked until their feet ached
became blistered and bled.
Franvera walked until the village
of her growing up became no more
than a smudge far below.

Now all she can see
is a warm red glow
on the valley floor.
Her mother woken by old Red Beard
joins her and together they watch.

FRANVERA What is that light?
MOTHER They're burning the village.
FRANVERA Our village?
MOTHER Yes.

FRANVERA   Don't – don't they want it?

MOTHER   They don't want us to have it. I haven't time to explain more. I have to go.

FRANVERA   Go where?

MOTHER   I must find your father – try to – bring him back.

FRANVERA   I'll come with you.

MOTHER   No. I will only be a little time. By daybreak I'll be back, and if I'm not, you must walk with these people. The old lady will take care of you.

CAST   Then come voices from the shadows.

CAST   You shouldn't leave your daughter.

CAST   What can you do down there?

CAST   I heard shots, I saw bodies.

CAST   Stay with your daughter.

CAST   Come with us.

CAST   If your husband's alive he'll meet us at the border.

　　　　　　　　Franvera sits in the mud and cries.
　　　　　　　　She can't believe what they are saying.
　　　　　　　　The old bread lady pats her head to console her
　　　　　　　　but she cannot be consoled.
　　　　　　　　In her heart she knows.

MOTHER   I'll be back soon

RED BEARD   Don't be foolish – don't you realise what's going on?

MOTHER   Let go of my arm.

CAST   Franvera sees in the light of the moon
　　　　　　　　that Red Beard is angry.
　　　　　　　　His face is twisted like an old piece of wood.
　　　　　　　　His coat is dirty. His beard is burning.

MOTHER   No one touches me. No one.

RED BEARD   We must walk – all of us, to the border.
　　　　　　　　There we will meet other soldiers
　　　　　　　　who will greet us and say,
　　　　　　　　'My friends you have been wronged.'

	They will take back our country for us.
MOTHER	That will be too late for my husband.
RED BEARD	It's already too late.
CAST	Franvera flies at the soldier
	her fists drumming on his coat
	her nails clawing at his face
	until she is dragged away.
RED BEARD	Hey – Little Red Shoes – you drew blood.
	That's good… one day we'll draw blood together.
	We'll be revenged you and me.
FRANVERA	Go and find him mother. Bring him home to me.
CAST	Franvera's mother does not know what to do,
	which way to step.
	Two days before she had danced in celebration,
	now her finger is naked.
	Her wedding ring lies cold in the pocket of a soldier.
	Her heart is an open wound.
	Her mind unclear.
MOTHER	He was so close – to walking out. So close.
CAST	She stops herself from saying more
	but it's too late.
MOTHER	Franvera?
CAST	They look into each other's eyes
	until Franvera cannot look anymore.
	There is too much to see.
	Franvera knows,
	In her heart she knows
	she gave her father to the soldiers.
	He'd be with them now
	and mother would not have to go back.
MOTHER	I'll be back by daybreak.
CAST	Then she is gone into the dark
	turning back only once.

CAST
The old soldier with the red beard
drinks and falls down in a heavy sleep.
His snores, sneak into the bones of the child
who cannot sleep, who waits for daybreak.

Now Franvera is back in her room
staring at the white paper on the floor
and without knowing why
she begins to draw
and in her head she hears
the sound her drawing makes,
the cries of the people
the commands of the soldiers
the words of the guns.
And her drawing is a house
and from its pretty windows
flames are rising –
red, red, red.

Now she turns and sees her drawing
larger than any drawing ever seen before.
It gets so large, it becomes a wall
so that her edgeless room
now has one side to its name.

As she stares at her picture
A light rises in the forest
and a bird is cracking open the day
with a dry throat.
Her mother has not returned
and everyone else has gone.
Only the soldier with the red beard
and the old bread lady are here.
Red Beard is still snoring

	an empty bottle by his nose.
RED BEARD	Where is everyone?
OLD LADY	Gone!
RED BEARD	Gone? Without me?
OLD LADY	Yes, without you.
RED BEARD	Why are you still here? Are you in love with me? Ha!
OLD LADY	She wouldn't go. She wanted to wait for her mother.
RED BEARD	Bah. You should have woken me.
OLD LADY	Nothing could wake you. You were drunk, you stupid man.
RED BEARD	Drunk? Not me. Drink doesn't affect me.
CAST	He wobbles from tree to tree
	like a sick goat.
RED BEARD	Stop laughing. Look at the sun – it's nearly noon. Hey Red Shoes – your mother is not coming back. We must go – walk to the border, the three of us, under the stars like – like the three wise camels.
FRANVERA	I'm waiting here for my mother.
RED BEARD	The soldiers weren't pretending you know.
	Soon they'll search the hills.
	Anyone left behind will be shot.
	You must come with us. Hey – tell her.
OLD LADY	Franvera, he's right. We must go now.
FRANVERA	My mother –
OLD LADY	Told you to reach the border – so –
	besides I'm old, I need your help.
FRANVERA	Mama…!
CAST	Her voice bumps down the mountainside
	carried on the morning air
	and Red Beard catches her from behind
	clasps his dirty hand around her mouth.
RED BEARD	It's better to have no voice
	than to bring death to us all.
CAST	The old bread lady hits him across his back

	with a stick she's found for walking.
OLD LADY	Leave her alone. Come child. We'll walk.
CAST	And so they begin to walk.
	Red Beard with a limp,
	the old lady, slowly
	as if every step was painful.
	The track is uneven,
	steep and full of stones.
	For six days and nights they walk
	until the old lady falls down
	and cannot walk anymore.
FRANVERA	What is it? What's the matter?
OLD LADY	My feet, my feet.
CAST	Gently Franvera takes off the old ladies' shoes.
RED BEARD	Why have you stopped?
OLD LADY	She has red feet.

RED BEARD What's a little blood in a time of war? Come we must walk till it gets dark.

OLD LADY I can't walk anymore.

FRANVERA Nor can I.

RED BEARD We have no food left. We must reach the border or starve to death.

OLD LADY There's always food.

CAST Now the old lady is on her knees
scratching around on the forest floor.

RED BEARD What are you looking for? A loaf of bread? Hey Red Shoes, look. She's like a big black mole, digging for worms.

FRANVERA My name is not Red Shoes.

RED BEARD Yes. I heard the soldier call you by name. He called you Red Shoes. He liked you.

FRANVERA My name is not Red Shoes.

RED BEARD Oh yes. You're well-known Red Shoes, dancing down the street, while your country was being over run.

OLD LADY Shut your mouth – she's a child. She didn't make the world the way it is.

RED BEARD What's that?

OLD LADY It's a root.

FRANVERA A root?

OLD LADY A root.

RED BEARD What do you want us to do with it?

OLD LADY Wash it, boil it, eat it.

RED BEARD Oh – yes, wait one second,

I will go to the kitchen to get a saucepan.

Oh look at this kitchen,

I didn't see it before because of all the trees.

So many pretty pots and pans.

Salt and pepper

and for the 'child' – Tomato Ketchup.

OLD LADY When I'm rested I can light a fire.

RED BEARD No! If we have a fire we'll be seen from miles around. The soldiers will think we're rebels and come to kill us.

FRANVERA Why?

RED BEARD Because they hate us, you stupid girl. Has no one explained it to you?

OLD LADY Be quiet – you don't talk to my daughter like that.

RED BEARD She's not your daughter.

OLD LADY She is now –

RED BEARD Yes, because her mother was stupid and went back to a burning village.

CAST Franvera is swifter than a cat

but this time the soldier is ready for her.

He catches her arms

and laughs as she spits in his eye.

RED BEARD That's right – now you feel hatred too. That's good – one day you will be able to use it, like a sword, a gun, a bomb.

OLD LADY Don't listen to him.

RED BEARD Alright – Alright. Your mother was brave.

She loved your father and went back for him.

It makes no difference – she's not here.

OLD LADY It's going to be a cold night.

> We must take the risk of a fire.
> You can hide the glow with rocks…
> the rocks will be warm to touch.

RED BEARD You've done this kind of thing before? Hey, old Mother?

OLD LADY Yes – when I was a child. But the mountains weren't as steep then.

RED BEARD Very true. I was a young soldier in those days. Very handsome.

CAST High in the mountains, they build a fire
and surround it with stones to hide the glow.
They boil the root in an old tin mug
but it never gets tender.
Franvera is hungry and cold.
The stones warm her hand
but the warmth is painful and she cries.

OLD LADY Be reassured Franvera, at this very moment,
not far away, over the mountains,
there are children like you, boys and girls…
watching television, doing their homework,
having a snack before bedtime.
All this will return to you, one day.

RED BEARD Hey Red Shoes, don't listen to the old witch. Why don't you tell her the truth?

OLD LADY Be quiet.

RED BEARD Oh yes – there are people, just over the mountains.
People like you Red Shoes,
watching TV, doing their homework,
but they don't care about us
no more than we ever cared about them.
Hey – I'm trying to educate you.

FRANVERA You said at the border, there'd be soldiers to help us.

RED BEARD Yes, the world knows we have been wronged. We will have our revenge.

OLD LADY   Be quiet, you sinful bag of bones. Don't listen – his breath is poisonous.

RED BEARD   I didn't have to stay behind. I could have left you, with little Red Shoes here to die in the hills but no, I stayed because I am a gentleman.

FRANVERA   You stayed because you got drunk and overslept. You stayed because you walk with a limp and can't walk faster than us.

OLD LADY   Hah!

RED BEARD   Hah!

CAST   Red Beard grins and lies down to sleep.

Within seconds he is snoring

as if he slept in a comfortable bed.

OLD LADY   Let me tell you something about him.

FRANVERA   What?

OLD LADY   How the old demon got a red beard.

Once long ago, when this war was young

he was caught by enemy soldiers.

They stabbed him in the leg

and hung him upside down to die.

That's why he limps.

But he did not die. No –

but the blood ran down his leg

down his chest and onto his beard.

It became red as you see it now.

He tried to wash it clean but he never could.

He gave up trying to wash it

and became proud of his red beard.

FRANVERA   Is that true?

OLD LADY   True enough. So – close your ears to his talk. His talk has kept this war going for a thousand years.

FRANVERA   I'm so cold.

OLD LADY   Give me your bag.

CAST   The old bread lady takes out the red shoes.

OLD LADY   Put them on.

FRANVERA   No – I don't like them anymore.

OLD LADY   Put them on.

FRANVERA   Why?

OLD LADY   Because I'm an old lady, and I deserve some respect for having lived so long. I would like you to dance for me, here in the high woods, like you danced that day for your mother and father.

FRANVERA   I can't... I can't dance anymore.

OLD LADY   Did your mother not say that I would look after you? Then dance for me – it will keep you warm.

FRANVERA   There's no music.

OLD LADY   "There was once a little girl

so sweet and pretty she was

and she loved to dance

oh she loved to dance

so sweet and pretty she was."

CAST   The old lady begins to beat out

the rhythm of the rhyme

with a stick on a stone

and Franvera puts on the red shoes

and dances just to keep herself warm.

As she dances – she becomes tired

and her thoughts wander down forbidden paths.

All around the edges of the edgeless wood

where the fire's glow cannot reach,

she sees black boots –

and the rhythm of the rhyme

forces them out of the shadows

because they too like to dance

and they want to dance with her.

How can she tell them to go away?

All she can do is dance with them.

She is exhausted now

and the boots are bold

treading on her toes
and still the old lady knocks
the stick upon the stone.

Now the black boots retreat
but Franvera doesn't know why
until she sees her mother and father dancing
together.
She rushes to them but they cannot see her.
Their eyes are only for each other
and they dance as they danced that day
so long ago
so long ago.

Franvera sleeps.
In the morning when she wakes
her bones are icy.
A pale ray of sun
cuts through the leaves.
Slowly she walks toward it
and it fades, returns and fades again.

She sees the room she occupies
and the paper lying on the floor.
She begins to draw the mountain,
and then the shape of the old woman
who once sold bread in the village,
who lies, still as a stone
in her black shawl beside the cold fire.

Now she hears a cry
and glancing up she sees an eagle
floating high above her
so very close to heaven.

It is so calm this bird
as if nothing had happened,
nothing had changed.
The eagle flies in her picture.
Now her room has two walls.
her drawings fill the air
giving it shape and memory.
For a moment she glides.
For a moment she's peaceful.
She feels as if she could speak
and be as she once was,
a child in a village
so very near, so very far away.

Now something crashes through
the cold glass air of the mountains.
Her heart and feet leap
into shocked space.
A sound so deep and piercing
it hurts her head, and she cowers
under the pale sky.

It comes again waking Red Beard.

RED BEARD Ha, ha!
CAST He has a child's face now.
RED BEARD Ha, ha!
CAST He jumps up and down.
His limp lends his fall
a strange rhythm –
He pumps the air with his fists.
RED BEARD Ha, ha!
FRANVERA What are you doing?
RED BEARD I'm dancing. I can dance too you know.
FRANVERA Why? What was that noise?

RED BEARD War planes.

CAST He becomes a plane.

He becomes a bomb.

Then he limps again.

RED BEARD They are off to kill our enemies.

They will bomb everything

factories, schools, shops.

FRANVERA I know why you limp.

RED BEARD Oh yes?

FRANVERA I know why your beard is red.

RED BEARD Then you, Red Shoes will understand. That's good. When the time comes you will know what to do.

FRANVERA I don't know what you mean.

RED BEARD Not yet, but there's time to learn...

Oh yes, this war has been going on a long time,

as long as I can remember... a thousand years.

Didn't the old witch tell you that?

That's how old I am – Ha! That's how old I feel. But I have survived. You know what you have to do?

Hey, Red Shoes, to survive this war?

You must learn to hate.

You must hate the people who killed your father.

FRANVERA My father is alive.

RED BEARD Believe what you want but you must hate. Your hate will keep you strong.

FRANVERA Does your hate keep you strong?

RED BEARD I am as strong as I ever was.

One day, we'll return to the village

you and me, and do to them what they did to us.

We will throw them out of their houses.

We will shoot the fathers

in front of their children. Ha, Ha!

And we will force the women

and the old ones

          to march across the plains
          barefoot to a strange country
          where they can weep for ever and ever.
          Then we can laugh again.
          Then we can sing our own songs.

CAST   But Franvera does not laugh.

RED BEARD Why are you crying?
          Because you're not very good at lessons?
          I understand. It's not easy to hate
          when you don't know how.
          Your parents should have taught you.
          You have to learn, like at school.
          Practise, practise, practise.
          Oh yes – I've been practising for a long time.
          Now I'm almost perfect.

FRANVERA Go away! Go away.

RED BEARD You don't appreciate me? Hey? You will one day, when we return to the village.

CAST   Another plane .

RED BEARD One day soon. How strange. Only an old woman could sleep through such a noise.

FRANVERA Wake up. Wake up! What's the matter with her?

CAST   The soldier kneels by the old bread woman
          and stares into her cold face.
          Then he cocks his head, rubs his chin.

RED BEARD We have to leave.

FRANVERA We can't.

RED BEARD There's nothing we can do for her.

FRANVERA What's happened?

RED BEARD If I knew that, I'd be a priest.

FRANVERA What do you mean? Why don't you speak clearly?

RED BEARD Because I'm kind. You liked her. She was a mother to you.

FRANVERA No – no! Wake up, wake up, wake up!

RED BEARD Hush now. Think of it like this.

She was older than the mountain.

The mountain was jealous

so it came and took her away,

as gently as only a mountain can.

FRANVERA She's so cold.

RED BEARD Death is cold. But we are still warm. Hate is warm.
Come.

CAST Franvera must run somewhere

run as far as her limbs can take her,

but old Red Beard is faster than he looks.

RED BEARD Stop! Stop!

FRANVERA I can't stop, I can't stop, I can't stop.

RED BEARD Take off the shoes. Take them off!

CAST She tries to take them off, but can't.

She struggles with them until out of breath.

She stops, bewildered, head in hands.

Again she tries to take them off

but the red shoes stick to her feet

and nothing she can do can get rid of them.

RED BEARD What are you doing?

FRANVERA I'm dancing.

RED BEARD Stop dancing.

FRANVERA I can't, I can't.

CAST She dances in the forest

and in the room where her pictures

are the walls and the doctor is there

trying to restrain her.

DOCTOR Franvera? Franvera?

CAST And Red Beard is there

trying to restrain her.

RED BEARD Franvera.

CAST She stops for a moment,

then the shoes take off once more.
When she wants to turn right
the shoes dance to the left.
When she wants to go up the room
the shoes dance down the room.
Dance she did and dance she had to
right into the dark woods.

FRANVERA Father? Mother?

CAST In the dark woods there are boots
bright and black.
Oh what a rhythm they make.

Now the doctor has gone
and old Red Beard is out of breath.
He leaps upon her, pins her down
still her feet kick.

RED BEARD Stop it. Stop it! Or I will chop off your legs.

CAST The shoes stops dancing.
Her body is limp.

RED BEARD What's the matter now, hey? You nearly danced
right off the edge of the mountain.
Lucky I was here to save you.
What do you think you are?
An angel?
You soon will be if you carry on…
What? You won't speak?
I don't care…
You never said anything useful anyway.
Come we must get to the border.
Come. Come.
Three days more.
That's all – and we'll be there.
You can't walk? Hmm – I will carry you.
Yes, even with my limp I am strong.

You know what makes me strong?

Ha, ha! Yes, you do.

CAST Now these two, are two among many.

stumbling out of the high mountains

beneath jagged peaks lost in sunlit clouds.

Some happy, some weeping

most just staring into the far distance.

Red Beard is holding Franvera's hand.

They stand at the border uncertain what to do.

Franvera has never seen so many people

so many tents, row upon row.

People talk to her but she does not hear.

She looks away toward the dark woods.

SOLDIER You've just arrived?

CAST Franvera stares down at his boots.

RED BEARD Hey – this man is our friend.

SOLDIER Who is she?

RED BEARD Tell the soldier who you are.

SOLDIER Why won't she speak?

CAST Red Beard shrugs, rubs his chin.

RED BEARD She stopped talking three days ago. I don't know why. Her name is Franvera and I have carried her on my back.

SOLDIER What strange shoes you're wearing.

RED BEARD Don't try to take them off, she'll scratch your eyes out.

SOLDIER Do you know her parents?

RED BEARD Her mother went back to find her father. A mistake. How many people are here?

SOLDIER Too many. Can you write? Fill in these forms. Franvera... there are children here like you. We will try and help you. There is a tent for you.

RED BEARD A tent? What luxury, hey Red Shoes?

SOLDIER   There's water, join the queue... food at six, join the queue. I'll send a medic to look at the child.

CAST   Franvera sits in the jaws of the tent.

People move by, some quickly

some slow as if they had been there forever.

but whoever passes by stares at her red shoes.

Red Beard fusses around the tent

setting up home – he whistles and sings –

RED BEARD   "Oh beauty, oh beauty when I saw your eye

that day when you were passing by,

two or three words I said to you.

Come here, come here to my soul

Because without you my life will be empty forever.

Two or three sweet words for the burning heart.

Together with everything else, I gave you my love."

Ha ha! Do you know what we are? Hey?

Don't worry I've been a refugee before.

People help, but the truth is

we are despised the world over. It's natural.

Never mind, it will make us stronger still.

Speak to me. Hey? Speak to me.

No? Then look at me. Look at my beard.

Good, I'm going to steal some food from someone.

Stay in the tent, better still stay out of sight.

Don't play with other children

and don't start dancing.

You know what happens when you start dancing.

CAST   He raises his hand.

RED BEARD   Hey? Yes. You know.

CAST   Red Beard wanders off,

limping down the long row of tents

smiling at people he is about to rob.

Franvera watches the huge camp
move from one moment to the next
until the sun has almost set.
All day planes fly overhead.

In front of her she sees a piece of paper
and she draws the tent
and the lines of washing blowing in the air
and she draws the planes
that howl and burn the sky.
Now there is only one edge left
to the edgeless room.
She looks up.
Some people are staring at her.
Children.
Children like her
who have seen things
children should not see.

CAST	Who is she?
CAST	She's the dancing girl
CAST	Her name is Red Shoes.
CAST	She's famous.
CAST	Hey Red Shoes. Would you like to play?
CAST	We can play soldiers.
CAST	Don't touch her.
CAST	Why not?
CAST	Red Beard said she danced an old lady into her grave.
CAST	He was just trying to scare us.
CAST	Why don't you speak?
CAST	Perhaps she can dance people back to life again. Can you?
CAST	Don't be silly, the dead have better things to do than dance.

CAST   Hey Red Shoes will you dance for us?

CAST   She frightens me.

CAST   She's only a girl in a pair of red shoes, come.

CAST   Please, come, come...

CAST   We are your people, dance for us.

CAST   Dance for your country.

CAST   Now Franvera feels
            the weight of her father's whistle round her neck.
            How strange that she should forget.
            Now she takes it in her hand
            puts it to her lips and blows.
            The people step back uncertain.
            What is she doing?
            Blowing a whistle?
            On and on, high and shrill
            like the cry of an unknown bird...
            Franvera stares past them
            there is someone coming.
            She knows his face. She's sure.
            Yes – it's him. At last.
            She sees her father
            and her feet rage inside her shoes.
            If only he would hurry.
            He moves so slowly through the camp
            stepping over ropes,
            ducking beneath the washing lines.

CAST   What's she looking at?

CAST   She sees someone.

CAST   Who do you see Red Shoes?

CAST   She frightens me.

CAST   Step back. She's going to dance.

Franvera's father is smiling
and although he has blood on his shirt
it does not frighten her.
Franvera embraces him
and they begin to dance
and the people in the camp gather round
and watch her dancing alone.

CAST   Who's she dancing with?

CAST   No one.

CAST   Now they watch sadly and say nothing.

CAST   Franvera is dancing for her country.

RED BEARD Franvera, stop, stop! Look what you've done. Now
you've started her she'll never stop.

CAST   Leave her alone.

CAST   Let her dance.

CAST   Her father's shirt is white,
white and red.
He kisses her
like he did that day so long ago.
He smiles and is gone.

Somewhere close and distant,
a whirr of wings
like a thousand angels. She falls.

RED BEARD Franvera! Franvera!
Don't leave me.
Open your eyes. Open.
What's the point of all this, hey? Our long journey?
If not for you? You know? For you.

CAST   She closes her eyes to his voice.
                Darkness flows in, an unstoppable tide.
                The world loses its edge.
                It has no shape, no line, no certitude.
                Now her arms and head are heavy,
                but she knows in her feet
                that she is flying, flying
                far above the map of her country.
                Like the eagle, so very close to heaven.

                Now there is a room
                with the walls she has made from memory.
                The picture of her house,
                flames leaping from the pretty windows.
                The mountain and the eagle
                and the old bread lady lying by the fire.
                The busy border camp, lines of washing
                and planes in the bright blue days of early summer.

DOCTOR   Franvera? Do you remember the day we typed your
    name into the computer?

CAST   Her heart quickens
                then beats so loud
                she feels all must hear it.

DOCTOR   Your mother found your name. Franvera?

FRANVERA   She's alive?

DOCTOR   Yes. She's alive. She's here. She's going to come
    and see you. As soon as she can – a few days. A journey.

CAST   The doctor looks tired
                there is something sad about his smile.

DOCTOR   Your voice?

FRANVERA   My voice?

DOCTOR   It's come back to us. I'm – happy to hear it.

CAST   She knows that he's kind
                but she does not know why.

Later, perhaps if she has time
she will tell him everything.

Now her mother enters the room.
How thin she looks, how pale,
like a ray of winter sun.
They touch each other's hands,
and study them for signs.
They look into each other's eyes
until Franvera cannot look anymore.
There is too much to see.
The red shoes are burning her feet
and she pulls away,
her mother catches her and holds on for a moment,
but the shoes are too strong.
Red Red shoes.

Time passes, as it always does
even in the worst of times.
Two years go by.
Two years and three months.
One day Franvera is at school
studying the map of her country
One day she is in the playground
teasing and being teased...
One day a week she talks to someone
in a room with her pictures on the wall.
One day it's time to go back
to another country
so very near, so very far away.

Now Franvera and her mother
are standing outside their house again.

The roof has gone,
the timbers are black.
There is nothing left
but dust and stones.

MOTHER   We will rebuild it – someday. Franvera?

FRANVERA   Yes, mother.

MOTHER   Do you forgive me?

FRANVERA   What for?

MOTHER   For leaving you, on the mountain.

CAST   Franvera nods, holds her mother's hand.
There are days when she dares not let go.

MOTHER   Franvera, take off the red shoes now. It's time.

CAST   Franvera shakes her head.

MOTHER   Soon then?

FRANVERA   Soon.

CAST   What happens next?
Is this the end of Franvera's story?
What does it mean?
Why can't she take off the red shoes?

Now there is a strange sight.
Here comes Red Beard.
He limps as he always did
but now he is wearing
a shiny pair of black boots.

RED BEARD   Ha, ha! Is it you? Hey – Red Shoes? Yes it is. Here
you are – oh look at you. I knew I would see you again. A kiss for
your old companion? No?

MOTHER   Who's this?

FRANVERA   He's an old soldier, that's all.

RED BEARD   Huh? Don't you remember?
I'm the one who saved you
when you tried to fly off the edge off the mountain.

I'm the one who carried you on my back to the border.

I'm the one who put you in the helicopter when you collapsed.

Where did they take you little one?

Were they kind to you?

MOTHER Is it true what he says?

FRANVERA Yes.

MOTHER Thank you for helping my daughter.

RED BEARD She's a good girl. I tell everyone her story. Everyone knows how she can dance. Ha! This is your house?

MOTHER What's left of it.

RED BEARD What happened to your husband? Did you find him?

MOTHER Yes. That's why we're here, to bury him and to have a proper funeral.

RED BEARD You are going to rebuild the house?

MOTHER No, we are going to live somewhere else, in another country.

RED BEARD Pah, another country, where they spit on you, if they let you in at all. How can they ever know what we've been through? This is your country.

MOTHER We cannot live here with our neighbours who did these things to us.

RED BEARD But you don't have to live with them.

We are throwing them out, every day.

Everyone who does not speak our language.

Everyone who does not belong here.

Hey Red Shoes, didn't I tell you

we would have our revenge?

Yes, even now they are leaving. Ha, ha!

They're afraid we'll do to them what they did to us,

so they are running away like dogs.

You don't believe me, look, look.

CAST   Now there is an odd sound.

People shouting.

Here comes a man with a suitcase.

He is pulling a child along with him.

They are being chased by stone throwers

who yell at them –

'This is not your country

this is our country

you don't live here anymore'

RED BEARD   Hey you, stop. Where do you think you're going?

MOTHER   I don't want any trouble.

RED BEARD   It's no trouble.

ANNA'S FATHER   Let us go, let us go, I beg you.

RED BEARD   Yes, it's a good time to beg.

ANNA   Franvera?

FRANVERA   Anna?

RED BEARD   You know them? That's good.

CAST   Now Red Beard has a gun in his hand.

ANNA'S FATHER   Please, please.

MOTHER   Come away Franvera.

RED BEARD   Let her watch. She needs to see there is justice in the world.

MOTHER   Franvera, come.

FRANVERA   What are you doing? Stop. Stop.

RED BEARD   You know what I'm doing. This is what we talked about in the mountains. This is what we walked for till our feet bled.

FATHER   I beg you please, let us go.

MOTHER   Franvera, come. We did not come here for this.

FRANVERA   I went to school with Anna.

MOTHER   This is not our business.

FRANVERA   She was my friend.

ANNA'S FATHER   It's true… it's true.

ANNA   Franvera –

FRANVERA She came to me, she risked her life. She came to me even though she'd been told not to.

RED BEARD Oh yes? You go. But give me that ring – gold yes?

MOTHER We will go now Franvera – bring your friend. It's all we can do. Come.

ANNA'S FATHER Yes – Anna, go with them. I will see you again. I will. I promise. Go.

RED BEARD Go. Go. Go.

ANNA No!

FRANVERA Let him go – let them both go.

MOTHER Franvera!

RED BEARD Now you make me mad! Haven't you learnt anything? Let them go? This man, who was your neighbour... who would not let his daughter speak to you? Who brought soldiers here to take your country, burn your house, kill your father, and leave him in a potato field to rot? Yes, that's what they did.

MOTHER Franvera – please, I beg you, come away.

CAST Now Red Beard is putting his gun to the man's head
and Anna is screaming.
Franvera flies free of her mother
and her fists drum on his coat
her nails claw at his face.

ANNA Father!

CAST Now everything becomes slow
as if time itself is tired
of all this hate and anger.
Franvera sees her mother
held back by people wielding sticks.
They turn on Anna's father
who raises his arms to fend off the blows.
But the blows never fall.

The people cannot believe their eyes,
they feel compelled to watch.

How could she dance at such a moment?
She tries to stop, but the shoes take off
and she cannot control them.
When she wants to turn right
the shoes dance to the left.
When she wants to go up the street
the shoes dance down the street.
Dance she does and dance she has to
And the dance is a struggle
simply to stay in one place.
The dance is a battle between
feet and shoes.
And her feet are strong
and red as the blood that flows
through her burning heart.
But slowly her feet begin to take command,
And then her dance becomes her own
and is beautiful.

Now Franvera feels the power she has.
The power of her story,
She is the girl in the red shoes
dancing for her country.
Everyone knows her now.
Slowly the group changes shape
they stand back to watch her
fearful in the face of her fury.
Only Red Beard is not ashamed.
Only Red Beard is not afraid.
He stares at Franvera
his beard, red as hell.
Now there is a shot,
and Franvera's feet
are no longer hers.

Red Beard's gun is warm in his hand.
Franvera falls, dances, falls.
Her mother is with her now,
her sorrow has no sound.
Franvera's feet are twitching.

Old Red Beard is falling to his knees.
He has broken his own heart.
He lifts his arms to the mountains
and wails like an infant.

Now there is someone coming.
Someone she knows.
It's the old bread lady
in her black shawl.
She takes off the red shoes
and Franvera is so happy to let them go.

A ray of light, so pale, shines down.
High above her, an eagle flies,
floating so very high
so very close to heaven.
Gently so gently she moves towards it,
and has gone.
Now everyone has gone,
and all that is left is the pair of red shoes.

The End.

Eye of the Storm

Eye of the Storm

When we are young it is a struggle to work out who we are and what we want to be. Throughout the play, characters claim to be who they are not. Trinculo, a sailor, pretends to be a duke, to impress Miranda. Stephanie, a girl, pretends to be a boy, to escape her controlling mother. Secrets are kept to avoid telling the truth. A seemingly innocent birthday present from Miranda's father, is in fact a 'tagging device' so that Prospero is father and jailor to his daughter. Prospero constructs a home on an island for his daughter, Miranda but he doesn't tell her about 'the world which lies beyond the mist' nor about her mother, absent from her life, since birth. Negotiating the parameters of freedom, safety and protection can sometimes misfire.

The set we used was an island construct; there was no attempt to pretend that it was a 'real' island. There were stones, which looked like books and a sea, which was made out of mirror, reflecting reality and illusion. The sky was created out of canvas roped to steel bars, conveying the feel of the wrecked and rotten sail of the ship, whilst also being able to convey the beauty of the natural world, thus making images, which carried a number of different meanings. We used puppets and projected images to tell the story, which heightened and illuminated the action. Through this form and the everyday 'masks' which the characters adopted, they were able to face the world and handle a multitude of complex life–like situations. The characters appeared in different forms – human and puppet miniatures. This conveyed the vulnerability of the characters when their miniature selves were sometimes faced with life-changing decisions. Throughout the play Ariel appeared in many different forms reflecting the ability to adapt and adjust, and become someone different depending on the demands of the situation. Her different guises also conveyed a strong sense of potential power.

Through these elements the play functions on two different levels, the 'real' and the symbolic. Combined with this, the characters shift from being one person to another, from one emotional state to another. The intention is to explore in an overt way, a number of questions: Why do we behave in the way we do? How does this behaviour manifest itself in individuals? Does it get us where we want to be? Does it make us the people we want to be?

Gail McIntyre, West Yorkshire Playhouse.

Eye of the Storm

Based on *The Tempest* by William Shakespeare. Commissioned by SNAP Theatre, directed by Andy Graham in 1993. The text as it appears here was re-written for the West Yorkshire Playhouse and first performed in April 2001, directed by Gail McIntyre.

CHARACTERS	**CAST**
Prospero	**Phil Jervis**
Miranda	**Lisa Rigby**
Ariel	**Ruth Dawes**
Trinculo	**Gavin Paul**
Stephano/ Stephanie	**Ruth Dawes**

The play takes place on a magic island somewhere off the coast of Italy. It is a place that reflects, in speech and costume a union between Shakespeare's world and our own.

ACT ONE.
SCENE 1.
A song is heard.

> Come unto these yellow sands
> whereon our play begins.
> An island rich, an island poor
> where Prospero is King.
>
> Now join we all our thoughts as one
> to conjure up our art,
> to tell a tale of sea and storm
> and many a troubled heart.

Voices whisper Prospero! Prospero!

Prospero's island. Midnight. Moonlight shines on Miranda, asleep. The gentle wash of waves can be heard and soft beautiful music. Prospero carries a long wooden staff.

PROSPERO   My daughter, asleep, her midnight eyes full of childish views, but tomorrow her childhood ends. Tomorrow is her fourteenth birthday and on that day I have promised to tell her the true nature of her past and how we came to live on this enchanted isle.
For fourteen years I have secured her here where I, Prospero, am Father, Lord and King. Once, in another life I was the worldly Prince of all Milan, but that was long ago.
 What manner of man am I now? I'm like no man you've ever known; sorcerer, magician, conjuror, scientist. All of these but still a man like any other. A father. In all my actions I am guided by the love I feel for this one being who dreams, at my feet.
This island is our home. It's a place of running streams, of birds and beasts beyond compare, wild woods, tamed by my magic hand. A sanctuary, where no harm may befall my innocent daughter. Oh she is innocent. She knows nothing of the world that lies beyond the mist that I have wrapped around this island like a winter scarf. Within its boundary I have created eternal spring. The power of my spell is such that no man may detect our presence here and I will jealously guard these shores even unto my own death. My spell will not be broken. Ariel?

Ariel at this time is a voice only.

ARIEL   Yes master?
PROSPERO   Is all the island sleeping?
ARIEL   Even the rock on which you stand.
PROSPERO   Wake me an inch before dawn so I may greet my daughter as she rises.
ARIEL   I will my master, for I am here to answer your best pleasure, be it to fly, to swim, to dive into the fire, to ride on the curl'd clouds…
PROSPERO   Yes, yes. Goodnight. *(He exits)*

SCENE 2

Midnight. A few miles from the island on the mainland of Italy. Trinculo, a young sailor pulls a boat to the water's edge. It's a small boat but large enough for a small sail. It's called, 'The Happy Youth'. Trinculo sings to himself as he prepares the vessel for sea.

TRINCULO   Ten gold pieces, ten gold pieces
              what would I do for ten gold pieces?
              I'd sell my ma, I'd sell my pa
              and as for my uncles, aunts an' nieces,
              I'd sell them all, cos I'm in thrall
              of ten gold pieces to call my own.
              But I'd never sell my love,
              for my love is as true
              as the salty sea, is blue blue blue–
              Oh I'd never part with her
              cos that's what love is... fer *(end of song)*
Ah love? What's that indeed but a poor rhyme?
Come on, Stephano. Midnight he said...
Why can't people keep appointments?

Stephanie enters, dressed as a boy called Stephano. On seeing Trinculo, she hides in the shadows.

TRINCULO   Who's there? Is that you Stephano? *(He looks, but finds no one)* This lad you see, Stephano, comes to me out of a dark night, says he has to run away from home. Run where I says? He's got no idea, so I says, 'Do as I done son, join the navy, see the world, learn a trade, meet some girls.' The Cap'n needs a cabin boy, a fresh faced beardless boy, and I need ten gold pieces. Well, that's a fair price for leavin home. Could say it was the 'going rate'. Ha. So here I is. Midnight by the water's edge. The King's fleet lies five mile out to sea an' I'm waiting on a lad who has most likely changed his mind and dreams warm in his bed.

STEPHANIE   Now perhaps, I shall change my mind. Go back, go home, go now.

TRINCULO   My nose is turning blue.

STEPHANIE   No, no I must stay, be strong.

TRINCULO   My gran, the old prune, always said we Italians feel the cold more than our northern neighbours.

STEPHANIE   I'll stay and tell you what's important here.

TRINCULO   I'm as cold as cod now.

STEPHANIE   This sailor called Trinculo...

TRINCULO   I'll give the boy one minute for every gold piece. After that, I'm home.

STEPHANIE   He's waiting on a boy who's not a boy at all. Not 'Stephano' as he thinks but Stephanie, a girl. I had no time to think of a wiser way. This is a desperate measure to escape my mother, and as for this Trinculo, he wouldn't row me one stroke from home, if he knew who I was, for he and I were once more intimate than now. But all that was between us once, as girl and boy, has gone. Be assured. How I shall maintain this thin disguise on board his captain's ship I have no plan. My only plan was to leave home, but now I'm nervous of it. Perhaps I should go back for this is reckless, and if I'm discovered – a woman amongst so many men, what then?

TRINCULO   Who's there? Stephano! Come forward, don't stand in the shadows lad.

STEPHANIE *(aside)* Forward then.

TRINCULO   Did anyone follow you?

STEPHANIE   No.

TRINCULO   Good. A life at sea awaits you, but first you pays the ferryman.

STEPHANIE *(looks at boat)* What's that?

TRINCULO   What's what?

STEPHANIE   That.

TRINCULO   Don't kick it.

STEPHANIE   It's got water in it.

TRINCULO   What's water to a boat?

STEPHANIE   Pardon me for saying sailor, but isn't the water meant to be on the outside?

TRINCULO   It's ballast. You'll learn all about ballast soon enough. Ten gold pieces.

STEPHANIE   What's this?

TRINCULO That's a bucket.

STEPHANIE A bucket?

TRINCULO You're so quick.

STEPHANIE Which bucket are we setting sail in exactly?

TRINCULO This bucket is important. You have to bail out the–

STEPHANIE Me?

TRINCULO Yes. You, have to bail out the ballast over the gunnel by the rollocks. Technical isn't it? Now I want my money.

STEPHANIE When. I mean, if, we reach the King's fleet.

TRINCULO If? If? How dare you insult this, 'Happy Youth' with an 'if'.

STEPHANIE Well?

TRINCULO I'm thinking.

STEPHANIE I'm sorry, I couldn't tell.

TRINCULO Hey! *(aside)* He's getting on my knuckles now.

STEPHANIE *(aside)* I overplay the part. Hold back or be discovered.

TRINCULO Half now, half on arrival.

STEPHANIE Done. May we leave?

TRINCULO We may. If we haven't missed the tide with talk. *(aside)* I'll have him, and his money.

STEPHANIE *(aside)* He's the same as ever, all pride and promises.

TRINCULO Are you coming or what? *(She gets in the boat)* By the full moon, you look familiar. Have we met before?

STEPHANIE No, for if we had it would have come to blows.

TRINCULO *(laughs)* Aye, ain't that the truth. Still I likes you well enough. Don't forget the bucket bosun. *(He rows)* What's the matter now?

STEPHANIE Nothing.

TRINCULO You're free in't ya?

STEPHANIE Yes. *(aside)* Too late to turn back now. The shore line fades by the stroke. What have I done? What have I done?

TRINCULO *(sings)* Sail away, sail away
what can I do but sail away?
So far from home, a man may roam
and may not return for many a day.

So I'll sing you a song
as we sail along
'bout the girl I left behind me.

SCENE 3

Dawn. The island. Miranda still sleeps as Prospero enters.

PROSPERO   Miranda. Miranda, wake up. *(She does not stir)*
   Ariel?
ARIEL   Yes master.
PROSPERO   Combine in harmony the sweetest elements of the
   isle, so that its song will, with gentle persistence wake my
   daughter.
ARIEL   It is done.

Music. Miranda wakes.

PROSPERO   Good morning.
MIRANDA   What time is it?
PROSPERO   Time to get up.
MIRANDA   Must you always wake me?
PROSPERO   It's your birthday.
MIRANDA   It'll still be my birthday at breakfast.
PROSPERO   You mustn't waste the dawn, especially when you're
   young.
MIRANDA   Let me sleep. Let me sleep.
PROSPERO   Miranda! Miranda! Get up!

*He bangs his staff on the ground, which makes an unnaturally loud
noise.*

MIRANDA   Don't do that. I hate it when you do that.
PROSPERO   Please, lets not begin today as we finished yesterday,
   in hot tempers. A new day, a new beginning.
MIRANDA   I'm just tired that's all.

PROSPERO   Then go to bed earlier.

MIRANDA   What have you got me? For my birthday?

He gives her a shell necklace.

MIRANDA *(flatly)* Thank you. Will you stop that music father? It's getting on my nerves.

PROSPERO   Ariel?

The music stops.

MIRANDA   Must she be here, always?

PROSPERO   Ariel, prepare a fresh spring for Miranda. Scent it with lavender and celandine...

MIRANDA   Etcetera. She's done it before you know.

ARIEL   Yes my master.

MIRANDA *(imitates)* Yes my master.

PROSPERO   She's gone.

MIRANDA   Has she?

PROSPERO   I don't understand why you find her presence so annoying.

MIRANDA   I can't see her. I can't trust her.

PROSPERO   Please try on the necklace. The shells come from the deepest part of the ocean, beyond mortal reach.

MIRANDA   So?

PROSPERO   Our need of Ariel is great. She knows this land and all its mysteries. She is the very spirit of it.

MIRANDA   I know, I know.

PROSPERO   When you were a child she was your constant friend.

MIRANDA   *When* I was a child.

PROSPERO   Treat her kindly Miranda, for she loves you as I do.

MIRANDA *(aside)* Every year since I can remember he gives me a necklace of shells such as this. It's beautiful, but the same present year after year must be greeted with the same smile. *(She turns to* *him)* Thank you for my present. It is really nice. I'll put it with the others.

PROSPERO   No. Wear it.

MIRANDA   Why?

PROSPERO   It would please me.

MIRANDA   Then it must be done. Now, there is some other birthday business to attend to? Have you forgotten then?

PROSPERO   No.

MIRANDA   This is my fourteenth birthday, isn't it?

PROSPERO   Yes.

MIRANDA   Then fulfil your promise. Answer all my questions. Why are we on this island? How did we get here? What's the world like that lies beyond the mist? Who was my mother and what happened to her? All these things you promised to tell me today.

PROSPERO   Miranda, for twelve years we lived happily here, but then, as if summoned by a bell, upon your thirteenth birthday you changed. Some awkward, confused and churlish spirit entered your heart. You are in constant opposition.

MIRANDA   This isn't what you promised to tell me.

PROSPERO   All day you sleep. At night, you force yourself awake, I don't know why, unless you prefer the company of owls.

MIRANDA   Oh yes... I like owls – they're a hoot.

PROSPERO   And then you wonder why you wake so heavily and discontent. You have become unruly, ungracious, unkempt.

MIRANDA   All the un words.

PROSPERO   And rude beyond compare.

MIRANDA   I have waited patiently.

PROSPERO   Patiently? You're not patient. Your days are too short or too long, too hot, too cold. Even the sea is too wet for your liking. When I offer you a remedy for any of these ills, you throw my advice to the winds. You are quarrelsome, untidy, ungrateful...

MIRANDA   Un, un, un.

PROSPERO   Insolent, moody, tetchy, self-willed and selfish too.

MIRANDA   Not to mention, bored.

PROSPERO   I had hoped that at fourteen years old you would be mature enough to know the answers to your questions.

MIRANDA   I am.

PROSPERO   Each day you prove yourself a child.

MIRANDA   Don't deny me Father, please.

PROSPERO   I have decided therefore...

MIRANDA   You promised me.

PROSPERO   To postpone this conversation.

MIRANDA   No!

PROSPERO   A year. *(Miranda screams in fury, stamps her feet and pulls her hair)* Be still, lest you unbalance with your fury the gentle fabric of the isle.

MIRANDA   You promised me.

PROSPERO   Be silent.

MIRANDA   Liar, liar.

She continues to rage. He points his staff directly at her. She stops as if frozen. The spell chokes her and she is in considerable pain.

PROSPERO   You are possessed.

MIRANDA   My limbs, my heart grow cold. Father, please... as I am your daughter...

PROSPERO   You have her face, her voice, but who you are I can only guess at.

MIRANDA   It hurts me Father.

PROSPERO   Then remember it, and when you see fit to raise another storm bear in mind the power of this, my staff.

He releases her. She collapses.

PROSPERO   Miranda...

MIRANDA   Leave me alone.

Exit Prospero.

MIRANDA	A storm? I'll give you a storm.
	I'll raise the waters from the deep.
	I'll turn the sea outside in
	and pitch it up upon its back.
	I'll howl into the winds
	and shake this island to its core.
	I will destroy the mud and rock
	on which it stands with my tempest.

Exit Miranda.

SCENE 4
On board 'The Happy Youth'.

TRINCULO *(sings)* Sail away, sail away
           what can we do but sail away?
           A youth may roam so far from home
           and not return for many a day...
           (stops singing)
  So, Stephano... Why run from home?

STEPHANIE Just row.

TRINCULO Course, you don't have to talk about it.

STEPHANIE No, I don't.

TRINCULO *(aside)* Sour little sailor in 'e? Still, I like the lad. Takes guts to leave everything behind, start a new life.

STEPHANIE It'll be nine gold pieces if we don't reach the fleet soon.

TRINCULO *(aside)* Or perhaps it's cowardice to flee, a failure to face up to things. Still, I like him well enough. There's something...

STEPHANIE Look, the sun's rising.

TRINCULO Do you really want to reach the fleet, Stephano?

STEPHANIE Of course, why shouldn't I?

TRINCULO Some lads find the navy tough. Tougher than home.

STEPHANIE Why should you care?

TRINCULO Oh I see. No one cares for you.

STEPHANIE Just row, or you won't get your eight gold pieces.

TRINCULO Eight?

STEPHANIE As the boat sinks so does the fee.

TRINCULO Well bail out quicker. Look, man to man, lad to lad, I lied.

STEPHANIE What about?

TRINCULO The navy. All you'll see of the world for six months is creaking timbers. You'll be sick as a dog the first week and treated roughly by the other men until you earn your self-respect.

STEPHANIE How should I do that?

TRINCULO Do something daring. Dive off the crow's nest.

STEPHANIE That's childish.

TRINCULO Yeah, but it's daring.

STEPHANIE It's too late to go back. I don't want to go back.

TRINCULO There's few comforts on board ship, Stephano, and most difficult of all, for boys our age, there's no girls. Mile upon mile of no girls. You have been warned.

STEPHANIE How do you survive?

TRINCULO I'm tough, in'I?

STEPHANIE You mean you don't have a girlfriend?

TRINCULO Oh I did, once.

STEPHANIE Of course, you don't have to talk about it.

TRINCULO Hah! There's no secrets in the navy. The sea is wide but the ship isn't.

STEPHANIE What happened then? With your girlfriend?

TRINCULO Not a clue.

STEPHANIE You don't know?

TRINCULO We went out one night and I was happy, glad. Next day she says she hates me, never wants to see me again. Complete mystery. Still… no skin off my nose. I didn't love her anyway.

STEPHANIE Did you tell her that you did?

TRINCULO Come on Stephano, you don't get as far as taking their socks off if you don't say you love 'em.

STEPHANIE You have no feelings left then – for this girl?

TRINCULO (*shrugs*) You ever been in love Stephano?

STEPHANIE Yes, once.

TRINCULO Oh yeah? What was she called then?

Low rumble of sound. Coloured mist rolls in.

STEPHANIE Listen.

TRINCULO What?

STEPHANIE I heard something… like waves upon a shore.

TRINCULO Waves? There's no waves hereabouts. We're in the middle of an estuary, twenty miles across. There's no waves.

STEPHANIE What's that?

TRINCULO Mist. Sea mist that's all.

STEPHANIE Looks strange.

TRINCULO Aye.

STEPHANIE Why are you stopping?

TRINCULO There's something odd here.

STEPHANIE What?

TRINCULO Listen.

Faint music can be heard.

STEPHANIE Music?

TRINCULO I've heard old sailors talk of such music, tempting a man to his ruin. An' I've heard tell of this mist an' all, which eats men alive.

STEPHANIE Sailors' stories, nothing more.

TRINCULO That's what I thought, till I saw that mist, heard that music.

STEPHANIE Well row by as quickly as you can. Go on.

TRINCULO Aye, aye.

STEPHANIE What's happened?

TRINCULO The sea is pulling against the oars. Look below.

STEPHANIE The sea, it's moving beneath us. Looks like… clouds.

TRINCULO Clouds? *(He looks up)*

STEPHANIE There is some storm beneath us.

TRINCULO   And above. Look.

Crash of thunder. A flash of lightning reveals Miranda standing high on the edge of a cliff, hair blown back by the wind. She is holding one of her father's magic books.

STEPHANIE   The sky was clear. I could see the stars, but now...
TRINCULO   Stand steady there, Stephano.
STEPHANIE   What's happening? Am I to be cheated of my life?

Crash of thunder.

TRINCULO   God in heaven. Give me your hand Stephano.
STEPHANIE   Give me the oars.
TRINCULO   It's no use. We'll be overturned.
STEPHANIE   Then we are drowned.
TRINCULO   By unnatural weather. We split! We split!
STEPHANIE   Farewell then, all my family. I have run too far from home.

A last crash of thunder. Stephanie and Trinculo embrace and there is a great sound of rushing water.
Blackout.

SCENE 5
Enter Prospero.

PROSPERO   Ariel? Ariel? Speak to me! I command you.
    You were but a breath of wind. I gave you voice and taught you human speech and now I bid you, make good use it.
ARIEL   Master?
PROSPERO   Who raised the storm against the isle?
ARIEL   Flesh of your flesh.
PROSPERO   Miranda?
ARIEL   Blood of your blood.

PROSPERO   But how? She could not... she has no power, no
  skill.

ARIEL   She stole into your inner cell and found your magic
  books and with them, conjured up confusion with land, sea and
  air. She made waves that would have toppled castles and drowned
  the giants who lived in them.

PROSPERO   Where is she now?

ARIEL   Hiding.

PROSPERO   Find her. Tell me where she is.

ARIEL   Master?

PROSPERO   Still here spirit?

ARIEL   She is so young.

PROSPERO   Go find her then or return in haste
            to the torment in which I found you;
            crying in the bark of a tree,
            weeping for release from the woody knots
            where cruel nature had imprisoned you.

            Ariel? Are you there?

ARIEL   Yes master.

PROSPERO   Forgive my speech, my daughter makes me rage.
  But go, find her and on your return I shall be calm and sweet as
  ever I have.

SCENE 6

*A beach on the island. Enter Trinculo. He collapses exhausted.
Stephanie enters, sees him and rushes to his side.*

STEPHANIE Trinculo. Trinculo, wake up. *(She slaps his face)*
  Wake up.

Silence. He opens his eyes and stares into her face.

TRINCULO   Steph...

STEPHANIE ano...

TRINCULO   Stephano. What's happened?

STEPHANIE I'm not sure. We were on the boat. There was a sudden storm. We fell into the sea, which was... was...

TRINCULO Wet?

STEPHANIE But our clothes are dry? Somehow we were brought ashore. I can't remember.

TRINCULO Oh God. Oh my dear... God.

STEPHANIE What is it?

TRINCULO We're dry. We're drowned and we're dry. Can't you see what this place is?

STEPHANIE No?

TRINCULO It's bleedin' paradise in'it?

STEPHANIE Well, it's very nice but...

TRINCULO No, no. We're dead.

STEPHANIE No, we're not.

TRINCULO As true as I was Trinculo, we're dead. We was miles from any shore. This shore line don't exist. We don't exist. We're ghosts. *(She kicks him in the shin.)* What d'ya do that for?

STEPHANIE We're blood and bone, aren't we?

TRINCULO Yeah? Then how come we're bone dry?
How come our lungs is empty of the sea?
Look at these trees, bearing fruit.
I thought we was in the middle of March.
I'll tell you where we are Stephano,
We're in the middle of nothing, an' I don't like it.

STEPHANIE It's not so bad. In fact, it's very beautiful.

TRINCULO Beautiful? I've seen islands in the Caribbean, what were beautiful, like this, but different. Bananas and coconuts don't grow on the same tree. We have to escape.

STEPHANIE In what?

TRINCULO Perhaps my boat has been washed ashore, same way as us.

STEPHANIE It's at the bottom of the sea Trinculo. Boat an' bucket both.

TRINCULO We'll build a raft then...with... with... with things.

STEPHANIE Don't sweat so. I thought you sailor boys liked a bit of adventure.

TRINCULO   This is no adventure – it's a nightmare. Listen, do you hear that?

A high distant whistle.

STEPHANIE   Yes, from over there.

TRINCULO   No. Over there.

STEPHANIE   Over there.

TRINCULO   Whoa!

STEPHANIE   What?

TRINCULO   Don't panic.

STEPHANIE   I'm not.

TRINCULO   Someone – something just ran its fingers through my hair.

STEPHANIE   They'll have greasy fingers then, won't they?

TRINCULO   I'm serious.

STEPHANIE   Don't be ridiculous.

TRINCULO   Ah! *(He jumps as the same thing happens again)* Devil where are you?

STEPHANIE   It was a breath of wind that's all. Trinculo, we must strike inland and discover if we're alone. *(takes a sharp intake of breath)*

TRINCULO   What?

STEPHANIE   I felt it too. There is some magic here.

TRINCULO   This place gives me the creeps.

STEPHANIE   Whatever it was meant no harm. I mean, we're still dead aren't we?

TRINCULO   Not funny.

STEPHANIE   Then come we must not delay.

TRINCULO   I'm not moving an inch. This beach is my home.

STEPHANIE   I'll come back then.

TRINCULO   No. We should stick together.

STEPHANIE   Then follow me.

TRINCULO   I'm not moving. All hell could be around the corner.

STEPHANIE   Stay then!

TRINCULO *(looks around)* Music, mist, devils, all this for ten
  lousy gold pieces. *(He turns, sees no one.)*
  Stephano. Stephano!
  Oh God in heaven, forgive me all my sins.
  Here am I, half man, half ghost
  unsure which half to believe.
  There's something bad here, unnatural.
  I can feel it in my bones,
  I was born with the instinct
  to know what's going down
  and here the downside is complete.
  This place don't smell sweet to me,
  it reeks of cleverness.
  (He hears Miranda approach, but will not look behind.)
  Ssh! Here comes a devil to take me off.
  I'm dead, I'm... dead.

He plays dead. Enter Miranda. She kneels by him.

MIRANDA   What have I done? Have I killed you? I have. I have.
  Forgive me. It wasn't me that drowned you, but my anger.
  Your loss is mine sir, for your face is the first
  I ever saw in all my life, except my father's. *(She weeps)*
  I so longed for you to come
  and this, your murder, is my welcome. *(She weeps again)*
  I didn't see your ship
  until I saw it duck beneath the waves.
  Why such a foolish, little ship? *(strikes his body with frustration.)*

TRINCULO *(aside)* Aaahh.

MIRANDA   Sweet face... let me see you. Are men so handsome
  then, even in death? *(He nods)* Soft lips, still warm. I, who will
  never kiss, will kiss you once, goodbye. *(She kisses him.)*

TRINCULO *(aside)* Like I said, nice island.

MIRANDA   Now I'll do my duty by you
  who's very presence in the world
  my father sought to deny.
  I will give you a rite of funeral.
  I will anoint your body with oils,

place you high upon a bed of sticks,
and burn you.

TRINCULO   About the burning... *(Miranda screams and backs away.)* Don't be afraid. The oils are fab... but not the burning.

MIRANDA   I thought...

TRINCULO   I know... I thought so too, but I'm not. I'm sorry if I frightened you. I thought you were some kind of demon. I mean, I didn't know who you were. *(Aside)* Oh, she's nice in't she? I mean she is.

MIRANDA   Who are you?

TRINCULO   Who am I? *(Aside)* She's well spoken too. Such attractive vowels.

MIRANDA   Tell me who you are, or I'll call my father.

TRINCULO   I... I... I'm – my name is – is Fred – Ferg – Ferdinand.

MIRANDA   Ferdinand?

TRINCULO *(bows)* At your service.

MIRANDA   You were on that little ship?

TRINCULO   That foolish, little ship.

MIRANDA   But I saw it sink beneath the waves.

TRINCULO   I was saved.

MIRANDA   How, saved?

TRINCULO   Not a clue.

MIRANDA   Then you're false. You're an illusion, part of my father's magic to test and trick me.

TRINCULO   I'm not false. I am Ferdinand, the... the Duke of Naples – as it happens. And you are?

MIRANDA   Don't come near me.

TRINCULO   Please, whoever, whatever your father is, I don't know him.

Silence.

MIRANDA   What's a Duke?

TRINCULO   Ah well, a Duke is... is a man of standing, power, money and land.

MIRANDA   You're real then?

TRINCULO   As real as your feelings. Touch my hand and see that I am real. *(She touches his hand)*

MIRANDA *(aside)* In all my wildest dreams,
I never thought that I would feel, as I feel now.
My blood races through my veins,
my heart beats in my breast
and my skin
is hot to touch.
I might call him a thing divine.

TRINCULO *(aside)* For some reason my mouth is dry.
Does a duke feel the same as a delinquent
when he meets a girl?
This girl is like no one I ever met before.
She's beyond words.
Most sure she is the goddess of the isle.

So, you live here then?

MIRANDA   Yes. My name is Miranda. I've always lived here.

TRINCULO   With your old ma... Father?

MIRANDA   Yes. Where do you come from?

TRINCULO   The mainland – Italia, Naples, Duke of...

MIRANDA   Naples? My Father told me of that place. A wicked place.

TRINCULO   Depends who you mix with.

MIRANDA   You must forgive my stares. You see... you are the first man I ever saw. *(Trinculo looks knowingly at the audience)* Apart from my father.

They stare at each other. Then as Stephanie enters, they kiss.

STEPHANIE   Trincul-oh? Excuse me. *(They do not break)* Excuse me in a louder voice.

TRINCULO   Stephano?

STEPHANIE   Oh. I exist... he looks at me, therefore I am. Who's she?

TRINCULO   Miranda.

STEPHANIE Pleased to meet you.

TRINCULO And I am Ferdinand.

STEPHANIE Ferdinand?

TRINCULO Yes. Miranda, meet my – servant boy.

MIRANDA *(bows)* Welcome.

STEPHANIE Excuse us, one moment, Miranda. *(She pulls Trinculo to one side)* What are you playing at?

TRINCULO Playing – exactly. I play the part of Ferdinand, a duke of Naples. I'm rich, I'm powerful and I'm –

STEPHANIE Lying.

TRINCULO It was instinct. She had this… smart voice. She is, she is –

STEPHANIE Don't tell me… you're in love.

TRINCULO No. Of course I'm not in love. I've never been in love.

STEPHANIE Not once… not you.

TRINCULO Not once, not now. A little confused, I'll admit to that.

STEPHANIE You're confused? I'm a ruddy servant boy.

TRINCULO It's just a… a part … you'll play it well.

STEPHANIE But still you have that look about… that look of –

TRINCULO That's not me. It's not me who's in love. It's this fellow, Ferdinand, you see?

STEPHANIE Oh...

TRINCULO The game's afoot. The hunt is on.

STEPHANIE Oh...

TRINCULO Play your cards right servant boy, and who knows… you could kiss her too.

STEPHANIE Oh… you don't mind sharing then?

TRINCULO Well… no, not really. *(Aside)* Oh foolish gob, what am I saying?

STEPHANIE So you just told her you were this toff Ferdinand, so you could steal a kiss?

TRINCULO Yes. *(Aside)* No.

MIRANDA   Ferdinand and Stephano. *(She kneels before them)*
Forgive me both.
My anger nearly caused your deaths.
It was I who raised the storm.
But you are both reclaimed, reborn, and I am happy.
So much more than happy now you are here
as real and true a pair of living beings
as ever an island girl beheld.
Now you must come with me.
It isn't safe here.
I must hide you from my father.

STEPHANIE   The man with the stick?

MIRANDA   Yes.

STEPHANIE   I saw him talking to thin air. Like he was mad.

MIRANDA   We must leave the beach. I know somewhere we can hide.

TRINCULO   I'll not hide. I'm a Duke... a brave Duke. I'll face your father.

MIRANDA   He has sworn to kill all who trespass here.

TRINCULO   I don't care. We'll still hide. *(They exit.)*

MIRANDA *(aside)* Oh brave new world that has such people in it.

She exits.

SCENE 7

Enter Prospero. We hear Ariel's voice, but do not see her.

PROSPERO   Have you found her?

ARIEL   I left her but a moment since, upon the southern beach.

PROSPERO   Then follow me.

ARIEL   My Lord?

PROSPERO   I will not wait.

ARIEL   She is in company.

PROSPERO   In company? Say, what company?

ARIEL   Two young men, caught in the tempest. Their boat was overturned.

PROSPERO   Young men? She's with them now?

ARIEL   She is.

PROSPERO   Have they done her harm?

ARIEL   How mean you, *harm*?

PROSPERO   Harm, as in *harm*. What other word would you have me use for the acts men are capable of?

ARIEL   No, she has not been *harmed*. They seem to be friends.

PROSPERO   Friends? How mean you, *friends*?

ARIEL   Friends, as in *friends*. They spoke together, and then fled into hiding fearing your reaction.

PROSPERO   Is she wearing her necklace?

ARIEL   Yes.

PROSPERO   Then we'll find her soon enough. But tell me, how did these young men survive the sea?

ARIEL   I saved them, as I thought just.

Prospero bangs his staff upon the ground and Ariel cries out in pain.

PROSPERO   All the infections that the sun sucks up
from bogs, fens and flats on Ariel fall
and make you by inch meal a disease.
I will wind you all about with adders
who with cloven tongues
will hiss you into madness.

Prospero points his staff into the air and we hear the snakes hissing. Ariel screams and enters.

ARIEL   My Master, release me, I beg you from my agony.

PROSPERO   You have disobeyed me, most wilfully.
Have I not been kind to you?
Did I not release you once from torment
even as I release you now?

He lowers his staff and the hissing stops.

ARIEL   Indeed, Oh man,
you released me, and then shut me in again.
You led me from one cage to another.
For you released only my shadow.
The rest with cruel magic, you withhold from me.
By your command I'm nothing but a voice, to all but you.

PROSPERO   All I've done was for the love of my daughter, and
of you. *(Ariel laughs)* Will you mock me?

ARIEL   Set me free, and I'll not mock you. Return my shape
and form...

PROSPERO   I have serpents yet within my staff...

ARIEL   No threat will I hear and no service will I give you,
Master until you promise, on your life, to set me free.

PROSPERO   Dare you rebel?

ARIEL   I rebel? Oh Prospero, know you not, this island's
mine?

PROSPERO   How can it be yours, foul spirit? You were
imprisoned by it.

ARIEL   Nature is not always kind.
Sometimes it seals its fertile self away.
Raging winds, drought and frost
fought for this island's soul.
I hid myself in a tree and there lay trapped
until your kind release. I thanked you,
and brought forth all the qualities of the isle.
I turned the brine pits into fresh springs
and I looked after your daughter
as she grew to womanhood.
From the cliff's edge and the drowning pools I saved her,
even as her own mother would have saved her.
Do I not deserve my freedom?

PROSPERO   My daughter has turned my reason into rage.
I am no tyrant, though you, and she, may think me one.
Do me good service, good spirit this last day
and by my staff I swear

that I will make the spell of your release.
Now lead me to her... Ariel?... *(Silence)* Ariel?...

He bangs his staff upon the ground in anger and exits.

SCENE 8

Enter Miranda, Stephanie and Trinculo. A sea cave, the light shimmers beautifully.

MIRANDA   Come forward, please.

TRINCULO   Where are we?

MIRANDA   Beneath the sea. The tunnel we came through
is, on a full moon high with water, but we're safe now.
I found the cave when I was a child.
No one knows of it, not my father, not Ariel.

STEPHANIE   Who's Ariel?

MIRANDA   Ariel is – a breath of air. A shaft of light. A spirit.

STEPHANIE/TRINCULO Oh!

MIRANDA   She's no friend of mine.

STEPHANIE   You said your father would kill us. Why?

MIRANDA   I can't explain him but you must fear him, as I do.

STEPHANIE   You're scared of your own father?

MIRANDA   He has powers you could not dream of.
But I forget myself. You must be hungry. *(She brings forward some strange looking fruit.)* Some food?

TRINCULO   Uh... What is that – exactly?

MIRANDA   Its a Lemato.

STEPHANIE/TRINCULO Oh?

TRINCULO   Course it is.

Stephanie and Trinculo take a bite.

MIRANDA   My Father is a scientist. He's interested in the cross
fertilisation of species. Nature is his workbench and his...

(Stephanie spits hers out.) It's a cross between a lemon and a potato.

STEPHANIE　　Tell him I can still taste the workbench.

TRINCULO　　Nah, It's lovely – spot on.

He turns aside and spits it out violently .

TRINCULO　　Lovely.

Miranda clears it away.

STEPHANIE　　Can't you stop lying? Or is it in your blood?

TRINCULO　　What d'ya mean?

MIRANDA　　My friends, my new friends.
There's so much for me to learn,
and for you to tell about the world beyond the mist.
We have all day and not once will our conversation cease.
My Father has told me so little.
He says this island is the real world and anything beyond
is like… like a waking nightmare,
that the world is ridden by plagues, war and famine.
He says that love has lost to hate,
that people are mean and cruel and never what they seem.
But even as you are my true Ferdinand
and my honest Stephano, I know he lies.

STEPHANIE/TRINCULO　　Oh.

STEPHANIE　　Excuse us for a moment.

MIRANDA　　Is anything wrong?

STEPHANIE　　No.

Stephanie takes Trinculo to one side.

STEPHANIE　　You must tell her who and what you are.

TRINCULO　　Why?

STEPHANIE　　Because it's wrong to pretend to be something your not. *(She glances at the audience)*

TRINCULO   I can't tell her now, it would only confirm her father's view of the world.

STEPHANIE   Then I will tell her.

TRINCULO   One word from you my lad, my conscience, an' I'll cut yer tongue out.

MIRANDA   Ferdinand?

TRINCULO   Hey ho?

MIRANDA   Will you fight? Over what?

TRINCULO   Over nothing. Forgive us, it's the way boys be. We fight and are friends again – it's natural.

STEPHANIE   You're not natural. What thought of you for her beyond your own desires? You disgust me.

TRINCULO   Oh? What manner of man be you? Most other lads would have clapped me on the back and urged me on to take my luck.

MIRANDA   What say you?

TRINCULO   Hey ho! *(To Stephanie)* There's something odd about you.

STEPHANIE   I might say the same for you.

TRINCULO   Don't be concerned Miranda. He and me will settle our disputes, later. First things first, sweet Miranda – your father.

Miranda backs away from him.

MIRANDA   My Father? What of him?

TRINCULO   We can't let him murder us. What's he called?

MIRANDA   Prospero.

TRINCULO   Prospero… I've heard that name before. Stephano?

STEPHANIE   I've heard the name but only in a story.

MIRANDA   A story?

TRINCULO   That's it… *'Prospero, the lost Prince of Milan.'* *(They look at him expectantly)* I know the title, nothing more.

STEPHANIE   The story goes that this Prospero, was clever but proud. He had many subjects and lots of land, all of which bored him beyond sense. His only interest was in his books, for they

were of the supernatural kind, beyond common understanding.
They say with his magic, he killed his wife.

TRINCULO   After which he disappeared, vanishing as if he'd
never been.

STEPHANIE   It's just a story Miranda... most likely not even the
same man you call 'father.'

TRINCULO   Don't cry, Miranda. Like he says, it's just a story.

STEPHANIE   Why shouldn't she cry? Stop telling her not to cry.

Stephanie comforts Miranda.

TRINCULO   Hey. Get yer paws off her.

STEPHANIE   Jealous are we?

MIRANDA   Will you cease your quarrels! *(Silence)*
I've often asked my father to tell me about my mother,
who she was, what happened to her...
He promised to tell me on my fourteenth birthday,
which is today.

TRINCULO   Oh! Happy Birthday.

STEPHANIE   That's not appropriate.

MIRANDA   You must help me escape the island by whatever
means... whatever it takes.

TRINCULO   Aye, we'll find a way. *(They hear soft music)*
Strange, I feel a bit drowsy of a sudden, so heavy with sleep that I
must sit down. What is this? I...

He falls asleep.

MIRANDA   Ariel!

STEPHANIE   What's going on?

MIRANDA   She's here.

STEPHANIE   Where?

MIRANDA   She's invisible. My father will not give back her
shape and thus he keeps her as a slave. Ariel?

STEPHANIE   Ah! She passed right through me, so it seemed and
left the seed of sleep. Miranda, will I wake or is this my...?

She sleeps.

MIRANDA   Ariel? Speak to me, you boneless, bloodless little
     creep.
ARIEL *(softly)* Miranda?
MIRANDA   Wake them, I command you.
ARIEL   When I've gone you may wake them.
MIRANDA   How did you find me?
ARIEL   Your necklace.

She rips it off.

MIRANDA   This is my place. Is there nothing, which is mine
     alone?
ARIEL   I've always known of this cave. I showed you its
     existence when you were a child. When you were my friend.
MIRANDA   You're not my friend. You spy on me, follow me,
     tell my father everything I say and do.

*Ariel now shows herself to Miranda. It's the first time she has ever
seen her.*

MIRANDA   Ariel!
ARIEL   I never told your father of this cave. For ten sweet
     years, it was our secret.
MIRANDA   How old you seem, how young. Why do you show
     yourself to me now, after all these years?
ARIEL   Your tempest weakened your father's grip
     upon the isle and gave me strength. For this
     I thank you.
MIRANDA   But what do you want?
ARIEL   Your father searches for you. I must lead him here.
MIRANDA   He's not my father.
ARIEL   He is so, and he loves you.
MIRANDA   Did he love my mother too?

ARIEL   I don't know the past, but of the future I can speak. Your Father has promised my freedom.

MIRANDA   He'll not give it. He *loves* you too much.

ARIEL   Trust him and he'll give you yours.

MIRANDA   It isn't his to give, but mine to take. Besides, how can I trust him anymore than you who will betray me?

ARIEL   I am your friend.

MIRANDA   Then don't lead my father here. I beg you... Ariel...? *(Ariel has vanished.)* Ariel...?

SCENE 9

MIRANDA   Stephano, wake up, wake up! *(Stephanie wakes up.)* Ferdinand... Ferdinand!

STEPHANIE   Wait, don't wake him yet.

MIRANDA   Why not?

STEPHANIE   Has the spirit gone?

MIRANDA   Yes. I must wake Ferdinand.

STEPHANIE   He won't wake to that name.

MIRANDA   What do you mean?

STEPHANIE   It's not his name. People, from our world, aren't always what they seem. He's not a Duke neither. He's a sailor.

MIRANDA   A sailor?

STEPHANIE   He wanted to impress you.

MIRANDA   Oh, he did.

STEPHANIE   No. He thinks you are a class above him. He thinks if you hear him talk like... like a working man – you'd judge him down.

MIRANDA   I don't understand. Why should I?

STEPHANIE   Because, my friend, the world outside is a very confused place. Men, women, boys, girls, the ties that bind 'em are all in knots.

MIRANDA   But why...? What do you want of me?

STEPHANIE   Nothing, except to help you.

MIRANDA   Then tell me his real name.

STEPHANIE   Trinculo.

MIRANDA   Trinculo, Trinculo. It tastes as sweet to me as
Ferdinand.
Trinculo.

She tries to wake him.

STEPHANIE   Wait, please.

MIRANDA   Why wait?

STEPHANIE   You've only just met him. You don't know him.

MIRANDA   I want to be with him, now.

STEPHANIE   I understand –

MIRANDA   Then don't try to stop me.

STEPHANIE   Did you not see, how he threatened me?

MIRANDA   I saw something else too, something deeper that's
kind, gentle and good. I love him.

STEPHANIE   You don't love him…

MIRANDA   Who are you to tell me what I feel?

STEPHANIE   I'm sorry I –

MIRANDA   My feelings for him, whatever he's called,
overpower me. But they give me power too. Power I've never felt
before because these feelings are my own and no part of my
father, I trust these feelings. They are indestructible.

STEPHANIE   And you think he feels the same way about you?

MIRANDA   Yes. Now let me wake him.

STEPHANIE   Sit down Miranda.

MIRANDA   No. *(Pause)* What do you want?

Stephanie lets down her hair and reveals herself as a woman.

STEPHANIE   You trust too much Miranda and you'll get hurt.

MIRANDA   Who are you?

STEPHANIE   He's not Ferdinand and I'm not Stephano, but
Stephanie. A girl. No boy at all, but a girl.

MIRANDA   You are all deceivers then in the real world.

STEPHANIE Like I said, it's all mixed up out there. People put on all kinds of guises, for all kinds of reasons. Sometime just to survive.

MIRANDA   You've lied to me as much as him. How can I trust you now?

STEPHANIE This lie wasn't for your benefit, but my own.
I had to leave home, the same as you must leave home,
but my mother wouldn't let me.
I could walk straight past her as a boy, as my brothers do,
and she would not lift her eyes. But if she saw me, her only girl,
she'd stop and ask me, 'Where you going Stephanie?' 'Who are
you going with?' 'What time will you be back?' You may think
this is a kind of caring, but that too is all mixed up, for who will
be my mother's company when the boys have flown? Who will
cook for her and carry all her cares? Me – or so she thought until I
became a boy myself. 'Oh,' she says, 'Go boys go, spread your
wings and fly… It's nature's way for boys to go exploring
but you my girl must do as I have done and stay at home.'

I will not. I have not.

MIRANDA   Your Father?

STEPHANIE Oh he went exploring years ago with someone half his age. It's not that my mother does not love me – she does, but her love, is like this island, wrapped in a perpetual fog. *(Miranda comforts her.)* Be my good friend Miranda and I'll be yours.

MIRANDA   Yes, yes. *(They embrace.)* But this, your story, doesn't change my feelings for...

STEPHANIE Trinculo.

MIRANDA   Whatever his name, his rank means nothing to me.
(She goes to wake Trinculo.)

STEPHANIE Give me one moment more.

MIRANDA   For what?

STEPHANIE For me to tell you what I know about – love, such as yours.
I was in love once, or so I thought, with a boy like him. *(Aside)*
So like him.
We went out together, and were as close,
as two can be, without becoming one.

The next day I saw him talking to his friends.
He pointed me out and laughed, and they all laughed
and slapped their paws together as if I had been the subject
of some bet or game, which he had won by my consent to kiss.
I felt betrayed, like all my feelings of love had been mistaken.
When I confronted him, he seemed surprised,
he said it meant nothing and was just boys bragging,
I told him it was over and he said he didn't care.
That's when I hit him.
He hit me back of course and then I lost control –
I rained down blows on him to match any tempest.

MIRANDA   Is your life, a normal life, in the real world?

STEPHANIE   Yes. This boy does not know what moves him.
He is driven by his peers whom he calls friends
to use you and to lose you. He does not care.

MIRANDA   Stephanie, you're my good friend and I've heard
every word, but Trinculo is different, I know it.
I'll wake him now, and in honour of your knowledge of the world
and the feelings in my heart – I will try him out.

STEPHANIE   Try him out?

MIRANDA   Shh. Pretend to be asleep and listen how he fares
with me.

STEPHANIE   And if he fares badly?

MIRANDA   Shh. Lie still and I will enter the land of deceit.
Trinculo? *(He wakes)* Ferdinand.

TRINCULO   Am I alive again?

MIRANDA   It was the spirit Ariel. One of her tricks. She's gone
now. Shall I wake your friend?

TRINCULO   No. Leave him awhile. The rest'll do him good.
All this sea air has tired him out.

MIRANDA   Alright. Well.

TRINCULO   So here we are then, boy, girl – island. *(He moves
toward her but she moves away.)*

MIRANDA   Forgive me Ferdinand, if I'm too slow for you, but
I'm confused. My father has made this island seem so real
and I've lived here without question but suddenly I have a

thousand questions concerning reality. Tell me truly, is this feeling you have for me – real?

TRINCULO *(on his guard now)* Yes.

MIRANDA   Then this is what's called, *true love*?

TRINCULO *(aside)* I hates this kind of talk. *(To Miranda)* Why do we have to talk at all? Words get in the way. Why don't we just be natural? Like we was before.

MIRANDA *(firmly)* Because I request it.

TRINCULO   Alright, alright. It's true love.

MIRANDA   What does it mean?

TRINCULO   What d'ya mean, *mean*?

MIRANDA   Please.

TRINCULO   Um, it's when two people look at each other and feel their love could last forever. Course, they don't know if it will, but there's a chance.

MIRANDA   Have you ever felt this way for another person?

TRINCULO *(aside)* I can't believe this. I've got all the ingredients– I got low lights, a cave, a cave girl, music. *(To Miranda)* Music?

MIRANDA   The isle is full of strange tunes, there's no harm in 'em.

TRINCULO *(aside)* And what am I doing? Talking.

MIRANDA   Tell me truly.

TRINCULO   Truly? Yes once. I felt love.

MIRANDA   Tell us – me.

TRINCULO   Her name was Stephanie. *(Stephanie raises her head in surprise.)* The female name for Stephano, as it happens. *(Stephanie lowers her head.)* But we split up.

MIRANDA   Why?

TRINCULO   Cos I was a fool. I treated her badly.
There's so much pressure out there.
All my mates were waiting for the day –
They laid bets on our first kiss, so did I.
Anyway, I never had the words
to tell her how I truly felt.
When she accused me of being bad to her
I became defensive, aggressive.

Where such anger came from I don't know.
Like a voice inside my head.
Now she's gone, a thousand lives away,
I'll never see her more is what she said.
What's up...? Seen a ghost?

MIRANDA   Nothing.

TRINCULO   But here, I'm different. Here I can, express myself. This is you and me. True love.

MIRANDA   And you'd never lie to me about that.

TRINCULO   I would never lie to you – only next to you. *(She moves away.)* What's the matter? Why are you crying?

MIRANDA   Oh Trinculo.

TRINCULO   Yeah? *(Realises he has been discovered.)* Stephano! *(He picks Stephanie up by the lapels.)*

STEPHANIE   What? Would you fight me again? Your Stephanie?

TRINCULO *(aside)* Oh dear. Oh dear. I am undone. *(He drops her and stands back in shock.)*

STEPHANIE   So it's love you're after now, is it?

TRINCULO   Yes.

MIRANDA   No.

TRINCULO   Shut up!

STEPHANIE   That's not what you told me, when I was a lad. Why, you even said I could share an' all.

MIRANDA   Share?

TRINCULO   Well... I – but it was – you – Ooops! But I'm changed. I'm different. This island... you... have changed me.

A crack of thunder.

MIRANDA   My father.

SCENE 10.
Enter Prospero. Thunder and lightning follow him.

TRINCULO   Run!
(He and Stephanie turn to run but fall as if their legs have no power. He turns to find Prospero standing over him with his staff raised.)
Kill me then. I am defenceless. Go on! Brave tyrant.

Prospero makes a spell, which renders Trinculo unconscious. Stephanie cries out thinking that he's dead.

STEPHANIE *(crawls to him)* Trinculo! Trinculo! *(turns to Prospero and Miranda.)* Is this your so-called father?

Prospero repeats the spell and Stephanie also collapses. Miranda backs away in horror as Prospero now turns to her.

MIRANDA   You've killed them! You've killed them!
PROSPERO   I have not killed them. What kind of man do you think I am?
MIRANDA   I care not. Get away from me. *(He grabs her wrist and she spits in his face.)*
PROSPERO   Who has fed you this hatred of me? *(He drags her over to Trinculo.)* This boy?
MIRANDA   Let me go.
PROSPERO   No doubt he professed undying love for you.
MIRANDA   Yes.
PROSPERO   And you for him?
MIRANDA   Yes.
PROSPERO   And with him you'd leave me and the island?
MIRANDA   Yes!

He lets her go.

PROSPERO   Where? Where will you live? On what money? Surely you've thought it through...? Food, shelter, clothes, a cot for the baby?

MIRANDA   Do you presume my innocence makes me stupid?

PROSPERO   Tis the nature of youth.

MIRANDA   What do you know about nature? Your island is nothing but a lie.

PROSPERO   Yet I shall be calm in the face of your contempt.
Your squall has upset the balance of the isle.
Step outside Miranda. See for yourself.
The trees are bare, the leaves fell down in one sad swoop
and snow begins to fall on all I have so deftly made, for you.

MIRANDA   I don't care. I'm glad.
Eternal spring was beginning to bore me.
Tis all unnatural – as I am – as you have made me.

PROSPERO   Is that why you want to leave? Because you think their world more natural than mine?

MIRANDA   Yes.

PROSPERO   Sad to say, it is not natural at all.
The words they speak, the moves they make each day,
from home to work and home again
in endless repetition until their dying day
are all controlled by magicians greater far than I,
being as invisible as our own Ariel.
Such men and women as these your friends
delude themselves that they are free at least
to fall in love with whom they choose,
but they are not. Love is not free Miranda
to wander between rich and poor
as water might from hill to sea, being *natural*.

MIRANDA   Say what you want. My feelings for this youth are beyond your control. In that, at least, I am free.

PROSPERO   What else? Think you their fashion more natural than mine?

MIRANDA   Don't ignore me!

PROSPERO   That his hair is short and hers is long
that she may weep and he may not

by some universal, *natural* command?
No. Tis all made Miranda, as this island is made.
From all their stupidities, I've tried to free you.

MIRANDA   But you haven't! You've imprisoned me, like Ariel.
Why don't you take my shape and form? Unsex me completely.
Isn't that what you want?

Silence.

PROSPERO   No, no.
MIRANDA   I will leave, Father.
PROSPERO   You love him truly then?
MIRANDA   I've said so.
PROSPERO   True love? Why, that's a powerful force.
No circumstance on earth could drive you two apart?
MIRANDA   No. So wake him and let me go.
PROSPERO   Indeed I'll wake him. I'll wake them both.

He makes a spell and Stephanie and Trinculo rise trance like and gaze into each others eyes.

MIRANDA   What are you doing?
PROSPERO   Let us imagine Miranda that these two are lovers,
and let us see together the forces, which act upon their natural
love.
MIRANDA   I will not watch.
PROSPERO   You will indeed, watch!

He uses magic to make her watch. Wedding Bells. Petals drop on Trinculo and Stephanie who, with the aid of a cushion, is now pregnant.

MIRANDA   What's this?
PROSPERO   Their wedding day and on that day
the heavens smiled upon them.
Now time runs on apace.

The child that was within, is now without
and the sailor home from sea.

SCENE 11

*Trinculo and Stephanie now act out a scene, which portrays them as
they might have been, had they got married. Trinculo enters. He's
been looking for work.*

STEPHANIE Any luck?

TRINCULO Nah, the port is packed with men looking for a ship
to build or sail, but there's nothing.

STEPHANIE The captain promised you work.

TRINCULO It's not his fault.

STEPHANIE Then who's fault is it?

TRINCULO No one's. It's the climate.

STEPHANIE What's the weather got to do with it?

TRINCULO The economic climate, stupid. Can't you keep that
kid quiet?

STEPHANIE No. Can you?

TRINCULO No... it's not my job. I'm going out.

STEPHANIE You only just got in. You don't think I need a break
as much as you?

TRINCULO What's hard about staying in all day? I thought you
women liked it. Eh junior, is your mum getting on your nerves?

STEPHANIE You've got no bloody clue have you? Have you?

TRINCULO This isn't what I thought it would be like. The three
of us stuck in here like crazy hens, pecking at each other.

STEPHANIE Then do something about it.

TRINCULO Yeah? Wave a magic wand?

STEPHANIE We have to keep our self-respect. We could start by
clearing up this pig sty. Bail out your beer bottles.

TRINCULO Here we go.

STEPHANIE I'm only saying.

TRINCULO I know what you're saying.

STEPHANIE I should know better.

TRINCULO   What?

STEPHANIE   Than to talk to you when you've been drinking.

TRINCULO   I haven't been drinking.

STEPHANIE   You're a liar.

TRINCULO   I'm going out. *(She grabs a knife and stands in his way)*

STEPHANIE   You think life is sweet for me?

TRINCULO   Put that down.

STEPHANIE   Stopping here month after month, waiting for you to come through the door all smiling and sunburnt.

TRINCULO   So you waited did you? That's not what I heard. I heard that my wife's been going out with every jack – o – the town. Now get out of my way.

STEPHANIE   And what if it were true?

TRINCULO   I'd kill you.

STEPHANIE   Yeah? Why then should I not kill you? Here, now.

(She waves the knife about)

TRINCULO   What you on about? Stop that.

STEPHANIE   You mean to say every time your ship drops anchor in a foreign port you don't go round the town with the rest of them, looking for girls?

TRINCULO   That's different.

STEPHANIE   Different?

TRINCULO   Cos I'm at sea.

STEPHANIE   You're at sea? Hah! We're all at bloody sea.

TRINCULO   Shut up! Shut up! You're twisting my words. *(He grabs her arm and twists it. She drops the knife in pain.)*

TRINCULO   I'm a man. A man has natural needs.

STEPHANIE   And what am I? A block of wood?

TRINCULO   It's true then? You've been with other men?

He raises his arm.

STEPHANIE   No!

MIRANDA   No!

PROSPERO   Ssh! It isn't over.

STEPHANIE   Of course it isn't bloody true. How could you believe it?

TRINCULO *(looks at his hand)* What am I doing? This isn't me.

STEPHANIE   You said – you loved me...

TRINCULO   I did... I do... but that's not enough is it? It's not enough.

He leaves.

STEPHANIE   Come back! Come back! Please... come back.

Stephanie is left weeping, and holding the baby. The 'play' ends.

PROSPERO   Is that the life you want? It beckons if you go with him, Miranda?

MIRANDA   This play, this mirage – doesn't come from them. It comes from you.

PROSPERO   It's a possible truth, that's all. It comes from my long experience of life.

MIRANDA   Is it also possible then, that something similar happened to my mother?

PROSPERO   There's no connection between these pictures and your mother.

MIRANDA   Did you leave her weeping with a babe in arms – while you voyaged round the globe being *natural*?

PROSPERO   *Miranda!*

MIRANDA   Is that why you've kept her secret from me? *(Silence.)* Then why? Why do you present me with possible truths but not, the *truth*? Father, this is where today began. Now tell me, who was my mother? What happened to her? Don't approach me. How may I grow up until you share these truths with me? Answer or I will leave the island and never see you more.

Silence.

PROSPERO   Your mother was the daughter of a wealthy man. She lived in a far away land where my father had trading interests. Her father and mine arranged for us to marry. We'd never even met. I was young... I knew nothing about women. I could barely speak her language. I didn't want to marry. I wanted to study my books but I submitted to my father's will. My father was upset when I showed no interest in his business but eventually we were able to move into the mountains to a castle where I could work quietly. It was a castle with a thousand cold rooms and towers so high they sometimes pierced the clouds. She lived in one tower and I in another. Sometimes I would hear her singing the songs of her own country and her voice would fly from one tower to another like a startled bird who flies into a room and cannot find the window again. *(pause)* We met each evening for a meal, and sometimes I would stay with her till morning. She was so excited the evening she told me that she was expecting a child, but I gave her little attention. My work was more exciting. I was close to great discoveries and I left her alone. It never occurred to me that she was ill, that loneliness and despair could make one so ill. After you were born, she weakened suddenly. I sent for a wet nurse to feed you and your mother was angry and didn't want to let you go, but I insisted. You were taken from her, as custom had taught me, and like a flower that sees no sun she slowly withered and died.

MIRANDA   What was her name?

PROSPERO   *Miranda.* It was only after her death that I realised what I'd done, and that I had grown to love her. I swore on her grave that I would do away with custom, and conquer nature too. So I brought you here. I know you can't stay. I know you have to leave and I have to let you go. I resist these changes only out of love for you and fear for myself, because then I'll be alone. My daughter, you are your mother's reflection.

MIRANDA   How could you have behaved so coldy? Why couldn't you see what you were doing?

PROSPERO   Even in the pursuit of good,
men are capable of terrible things.
From this truth and a thousand others
I have tried to protect you.
Perhaps wrongly, selfishly.

Whether tis in our nature or in our circumstance
you must discern for yourself. *(She weeps.)*
Miranda? Forgive me.

She goes to him. They embrace. We hear Ariel's voice.

ARIEL   My Lord?

PROSPERO   Ariel?

ARIEL   The island has forgot which season it is in.
The snow falls, then stops and falls again.
The spring buds wake and stretch
and then retract, if they can,
or else stand frozen at the gate.
It's January and June all in a glance,
and destruction can but follow
unless you unravel all your spells.

PROSPERO   I shall. I must see to this.
Wake your friends Miranda. Don't be afraid.
They won't recall the parts they played.
They were such stuff as dreams are made on… Farewell.

MIRANDA   Father?

PROSPERO   Go safely Miranda.

Exit Prospero. Miranda wakes Trinculo and Stephanie.

TRINCULO   What's happened?

STEPHANIE Where's your Father ?

MIRANDA   All's well.

STEPHANIE Are you alright?

MIRANDA   Yes.

TRINCULO   Miranda, I must talk to you.

MIRANDA   Not now. Now we must find some way of leaving
the island.

We hear Ariel's voice.

ARIEL   Miranda.

MIRANDA   Spirit?

ARIEL   Your father sends me back. To see you safely from this rock is my last service.

MIRANDA   Will you be free then?

ARIEL   As free as I may be, within the confines of this isle. Now come. He bade me promise you auspicious gales and calm seas.

MIRANDA   We'll follow then.

TRINCULO   But we've nothing to sail in.

STEPHANIE   Your father's going to help us?

MIRANDA   Yes.

STEPHANIE   Why?

TRINCULO   It could be a trick.

MIRANDA   I'll explain…

ARIEL   Be swift and follow me.

MIRANDA   …later…

Exit all.

SCENE 12

Music, which indicates that Prospero has restored harmony to the island. Enter Prospero.

PROSPERO   Auspicious gales and calm seas.
    These I can only offer for a time
    after which your life, like your little boat
    is open to all kinds of rough weather.
    I know she is a woman now,
    but I cannot help, but see her as she was.
    A child, who came to me
    with every scrape of the knee.
    Who wept and laughed and grew
    within the warm embrace of my eyes.
    And now she goes – is gone. Ariel?

ARIEL *(Voice over)* Yes master?

PROSPERO   Have you done as I asked?

ARIEL *(Voice over)* They're running to the beach at full youthful
speed.

PROSPERO   And the sea?

ARIEL *(Voice over)* Is calm, though they've enough wind
to stand in the shoulder of a sail.

PROSPERO   Farewell then Spirit,
and with this spell I thee untie.
Forgive me now, before you fly
if ever Prospero has been unkind.

ARIEL *(Voice over, laughs)* Farewell Master…
(A sound and light that diminishes as she goes)
Farewell… farewell… farewell…

PROSPERO   Farewell then, without forgiveness.
Have I not been a fair Master and an honest Father?
The future will judge a parent best,
for how our children treat their own
is the truest reflection of our care.
(Silence. Prospero is exhausted.)
Now my charms are all o'er thrown
and what strength I have's mine own
which is most faint.

Prospero stands at the cliff's edge looking over the sea.

SCENE 13

*Enter Trinculo, Miranda and Stephanie at pace. The boat has
reappeared.*

TRINCULO   My boat! My boat and my bucket both.
Oh *Happy Youth*! Now this is magic.

STEPHANIE   Come Miranda, don't stand upon the shore.

MIRANDA   Yes I'll come, but let me take one last look.
My childhood is in these grains of sand
these rocks, this island air.

TRINCULO   Speakin' as a sailor, the sea's as good for an honest
boat as I ever saw. So come, the tide will turn eventually.

MIRANDA   Goodbye Father... Goodbye Ariel.

We hear the soft echo of Ariel's 'Farewell'.

STEPHANIE   Hurry. *(Miranda turns to the boat but stops.)* What's the matter?

TRINCULO   Miranda?

MIRANDA   I can't.

TRINCULO   Why not?

MIRANDA   I'm afraid of the life that awaits me.

STEPHANIE   Listen to me. I'll return home, face my family and speak my mind as you have done. This help you've given me and I'll help you.

TRINCULO   And so will I, as kindly as I can.
I'm changed Miranda. I am.
Will a man not change who has been drowned
and given a second life? *(Miranda gets in the boat.)*
That's the spirit.

STEPHANIE   My good friend.

TRINCULO   But wait. What about my ten gold pieces? You owe me.

STEPHANIE   What about the apology, you owe me?

TRINCULO   I owe you more than that. *(He offers his hand and she takes it.)* Seven gold pieces?

STEPHANIE   Just row.

TRINCULO   A joke, a jest.

MIRANDA *(aside)* With every stroke of the oar I'm more alone,
more uncertain and yet more alive.
My father did confine me
but now his gentle breath fills our sail.
My questions all seem answered
but these remain. Who am I? Where am I going?

She puts on the necklace once again, which was her father's birthday gift.

Song.

> Full fathom five, thy Father lies.
> Those are pearls that were his eyes.
> Nothing of him that doth fade
> but doth suffer a sea change
> Into some thing rich and strange.

Lights fade down.
The End.

Playing from the Heart

Playing from the Heart

As Artistic Director of Polka Theatre for Children, I often commission new plays and thinking of suitable subjects is one of my most difficult, yet rewarding tasks. I had long been fascinated by Evelyn Glennie, both as an extraordinary person and as an amazing musician and I started to think about the journey she had made to become the world's leading percussionist. I realised that in the way Evelyn approached and overcame what many would regard as a huge obstacle to becoming a musician – her profound deafness – she was a role model for children.

I was convinced that there was a play there; a play with the qualities of a tone poem and I had no doubts about whom to approach with the idea. Charles Way is one of my favourite writers for children and I felt if anybody could create such a play, he could.

Evelyn was delighted with the idea and allowed us to use her autobiography as a starting point. She and Charles then had a long and interesting meeting in the café of the Birmingham Symphony Hall. It was very noisy, which made it difficult for him, but of course it was perfectly easy for her – it was silent, and, as they talked and Evelyn lip-read, Charles realised that words for her are shapes, not sounds. He went on from there to explore the practical difficulties and possibilities associated with deafness from the point of view that all sounds can also be seen or felt.

We then held script workshops to develop ideas, visited Evelyn's concerts and spent time in her music workshop. The more we got to know her, the more we understood her desire to communicate to young people the power of music and especially, of percussion.

As Charles worked, he felt he was writing not so much a play, more a theatre event with the structure of an extended piece of music. As the play evolved, I became more and more excited by his creation. Evelyn came to rehearsals to help and encourage. Thus the play was created – a fusion of words, emotions and music.

Enormous thanks to Evelyn, who allowed us to use her extraordinary story, to all involved in the initial project who gave from the heart to make it happen but especially to Charles who took the idea and gave it wings. He has created a beautiful and moving play that speaks to all young people about courage and artistry. I cannot thank him enough. **Vicky Ireland, Polka Theatre.**

Playing from the Heart.

A theatre event based on the early life of Evelyn Glennie.
With thanks to Evelyn Glennie.

The play was first commissioned by Polka Theatre for Children, Wimbledon, London where it was directed by Vicky Ireland, in October 1998. Designed by Ruth Finn and Gary Thorne, with music by Andrew Dodge and Craig Vear, it was performed with the following cast:

CHARACTERS	CAST
Evelyn	Louise Bolton
Mum	Lesley Stone
Dad	Iain Stuart Robertson
Colin	James D McKechnie
Roger	Brian Timoney

The cast may also play a number of other roles including:

Mrs Rachlin
Reporter
Photographer
Editor
Teacher
Doctor 1
Doctor 2
Careers Officer
Woman
Floss the dog

The play is set in Scotland. The action of the play takes place in various settings, which may be suggested minimally, and non realistically The set can be thought of as one large percussive opportunity.

ACT ONE

Darkness. Sound of an orchestra tuning up. Light rises on a young woman in a concert dress: Evelyn. A single pure note.

EVELYN   I can hear you thinking –
                I can hear you thinking –
                What's going on?
                What on earth is she about to do –
                This girl in a party dress?
                This is it, you see.
                The moment.
                All my life I've worked
                for this moment.
                They say I will never be a musician
                today I will prove them wrong.
                This is it.
                The orchestra's ready.
                The audience applaud
                as the conductor walks
                in his black suit across the stage.
                I feel his steps
                in the wood beneath my feet.
                I feel the sound of clapping
                in the tense air of the concert hall.
                I watch the faces of the people,
                the movement of their hands.

                Of course it could all go wrong.
                I could lose my way
                In the great forest of notes.
                No! I must concentrate.
                I must succeed.
                I will succeed.
                I am me –
                Me is a very determined person.
                This is it – the moment.
                The conductor raises his baton,
                The audience breathe in –

(An intake of air)
– the baton hovers in the air
Holding time
Holding time.
A bead of sweat runs down
the conductor's cheek.
How slowly it falls...
How slowly...
(Sound of heart beat)
But wait!
What's happening?
What sound is that?
The sound of my heart
slowing down...
slowing down...

She approaches the conductor who is now frozen in time. She moves around the orchestra, then she hears whispers, voices from her childhood.

EVELYN   Wait! What sound is that?
The sound of my thoughts
running back, running back
to the place of beginning –
the place where my heart
learnt its sure rhythm. Home.
Home. Come with me.
It will only take a moment...

The conductor / orchestra ensemble break out of their frozen positions. A movement section follows – transforming them into the characters in Evelyn's life. She is whisked out of her party dress. She is now eight years old wearing wellies and a duffle coat and a bobble hat.

EVELYN   When I was a child I lived on a farm.
When I was a child
I climbed the grain tower

it was ever so high.
Tall as a tower
in a fairy story.
When I was a child
I had a red wheelbarrow.
There it is.
When I was a child
We had a dog called Floss.
There she is.
When I was eight years old
I climbed to the top of the grain tower...
(Sound of wind)
I tried to pull down clouds.
When I was child
I could hear fields waking up
stretching their muddy arms.
I could hear the wind
comb the long grass all day.
I could hear the world sigh
at four o'clock
and the slow breathing of the earth
at night.

From the top of the tower
I could see the whole farm
and beyond the farm – the fields
beyond the fields
the future...
When I was a child
I climbed to the top of the grain tower
and was queen of everything I saw...

Mum enters.

MUM	Evelyn.
EVELYN	That's my mother.
MUM	What are you doing?

EVELYN   I'm fine.

MUM   You'll be fine down here too on solid ground. Get down! Get down.

EVELYN   But her voice was blown away –

Dad enters with dog.

DAD   What now?

MUM   Evelyn's climbed to the top of the grain tower.

DAD   It's not the first time.

Floss the dog follows the father around everywhere – the dog belongs to him.

EVELYN   My father –

MUM   She's only eight.

DAD   Old enough to climb up, old enough to climb down.

MUM   It's thirty feet.

DAD   Aye. It's a tall tower.

EVELYN   Thirty feet up – a girl in the sky. Look Mum! *(Mum screams)* No hands.

DAD   She's testing herself.

MUM   She's testing me.

EVELYN   I'm testing myself.

MUM   Come down now.

DAD   She'll come down –

MUM   Where are you going?

DAD   I have to feed the pigs.

MUM   *Pigs*, you care more about the pigs than your daughter up the grain tower.

DAD   That isn't true.
I care more about you
than I care about the pigs
and I care about the pigs
a great deal.

MUM   Oh flattered I am.

He grabs her momentarily and they waltz in their work clothes.

EVELYN   My parents – dancing in the yard
                 Very strange.
                 I watch them from the grain tower –
                 My Mother
                 full of fret
                 worrying about the future –
                 her movements quick, busy.
MUM   Go on feed the pigs, before I fall down dizzy.
EVELYN   My Father always walks at the same pace
his movements measured,
appearing calm... It's a trick.
He says...
DAD   Patience is a virtue.

Enter two brothers, chasing each other.

DAD   Slow down there.
COLIN   Why?
DAD   Why? Why indeed? Why not?

Father moves away. The boys resume their chase, which develops into a pattern.

EVELYN   Two brothers,
                 chalk and cheese
                 cheese and chalk –
                 different,
                 like low ground
                 and high ground
                 like loud and quiet
                 always fighting
                 cat and dog.
DAD *(to Colin and Roger)* Stop that!

MUM	Evelyn – get down.
EVELYN	My family.

Evelyn beats out a rhythm on the grain tower – initiating a movement section that is about the family: love, reprimands, patterns of behaviour and support. It stops suddenly. Silence. Evelyn comes down.

EVELYN	My ears hurt.
MUM	What kind of hurt?
EVELYN	The kind that hurts.
MUM	I'm not surprised hanging up there in the sky in a howling wind, letting the whole of Scotland blow right through you.
COLIN	She's always complaining about her ears –
EVELYN	No I'm not.
COLIN	Are too.
EVELYN	Not.
ROGER	You said your ears hurt yesterday.
COLIN	After riding your bike.
ROGER	In the cold.
COLIN	And after swimming.
EVELYN	They just hurt, that's all.
COLIN	You're going deaf.
EVELYN	No, I'm not.
COLIN	Are too.
EVELYN	Stop saying that.
COLIN	Sometimes I speak to you and you don't hear a word I say.
EVELYN	That's cos all you say is – 'Are too! Are too!'
COLIN	No, I don't.
EVELYN	Do too! Do too!
MUM	Stop!
EVELYN	I'm not going deaf, am I Mum?

MUM	Course not – just got sore ears, that's all. But stay out of the cold wind and don't dive down deep in the swimming pool.
EVELYN	OOOh. *(in disappointment)*
DAD	Hush now... Hush – feel that?
MUM	What?
DAD	That.
MUM	That what?
DAD	Something's coming.
MUM	What's coming?
DAD	Wait... there... it's arrived.
MUM	What?
DAD	The summer... *(Lights change)* I can feel it in my bones smell it on the breeze. Besides it says so in the paper – Today is the first day of summer – official.

He exits. The youngsters stand perplexed.

MUM	Stop arguing.
ROGER	We're not arguing.
MUM	You think I can't tell an argument when I hear one? Silent or not.

She exits. The summer light gets stronger.

COLIN	I love the summer.
ROGER	We could put a tent up.
COLIN	Yeah, spend the night in the garden.
EVELYN	And me.
COLIN	Not you
ROGER	You're too young.
EVELYN	No I'm not.
ROGER	You're afraid of the dark.

EVELYN	That's a secret.
COLIN	Not anymore.
EVELYN	Stop it.
ROGER.	What?
EVELYN	Teasing.
ROGER/COLIN	Tarenzeening.
EVELYN	Please?
COLIN	No.
EVELYN	I'll tell on you.
COLIN	Tell what?
ROGER	There's nothing to tell.
EVELYN	I'll make it up.
ROGER	You wouldn't dare.
EVELYN	I always dare.

Silence.

ROGER   Alright.

They set up the tent – this action demonstrates their rivalry and affection – it's comic and musical. Roger is the practical one, Colin more of a dreamer. Night falls.

EVELYN   I love my brothers
                I hate my brothers
                I love my brothers.

In the tent: Roger is making a lego plane, Colin is reading.

COLIN   I'm going to be an astronaut.
EVELYN   When?
COLIN   When I'm grown up, like the man in this book. He
  goes to different planets.
EVELYN   What for?
COLIN   To see what's there.

ROGER   I'm going to be a farmer, like dad. What are you
   going to do Ev?
EVELYN   Don't know…

She decides to beat a toy drum.

COLIN   Shh!
EVELYN   Why shh?
COLIN   I'm trying to read.
EVELYN   Try harder. *(She plays on)*
ROGER   Shh.
EVELYN   Why shh?
ROGER   I can't hear myself think.
EVELYN   Think louder. *(She plays on)*
COLIN/ROGER Shh!

*She plays louder. Colin storms off, comes back with a trombone . He
creeps up behind Evelyn and blows it in her ear. She screams. Roger
falls about laughing, Evelyn hits him. Colin hides the drum.*

EVELYN   Where is it?
COLIN   Where's what?
EVELYN   My drum.
COLIN   I never saw a drum. Did you see a drum?
ROGER   Well it was – no, no.
EVELYN *(picks up plane)* Did you ever see a plane with one wing?
ROGER   You wouldn't dare.

*She snaps off the wing. She picks up Colin's book and is about to rip
it in two. Colin swiftly gives the drum back.*

EVELYN   I'm going to be a musician.
ROGER   You broke my plane. *(He hits her with a pillow.)*
EVELYN   You stole my drum.
ROGER   He stole your drum.

COLIN	It's not my fault she broke your stupid plane.
ROGER	It's not stupid.
COLIN	It is now – it's only got one wing.

A pillow fight develops between the two brothers. Enter Mum with rolled up newspaper.

MUM	Stop! Stop! You will stop that now.

They continue. Evelyn stands by in an innocent pose.

MUM	Stop!

She starts to chase them with the rolled up newspaper. Dad enters with the dog, barking – chaos.

COLIN	She started it.
EVELYN	I never did.
ROGER	She did! She did!
EVELYN	I hate my brothers
	I love my brothers
	I hate my brothers.

The scene changes, folds into a new section. Evelyn gets on her bicycle.

MUM	If you three could sell arguments, you'd be millionaires.
EVELYN	It *was* true.
MUM	And I don't want to hear who started it.
EVELYN	It was never me.
MUM	It's always someone else.
EVELYN	And father used to say –
DAD	Three is an argumentative number.
MUM	Evelyn… slow down on that bicycle.

She peddles faster. She peddles through the seasons – summer lights fade.

EVELYN   Whole seasons passed in squabbles.
It was great. And I would ride my bike
through the changing year
watching the leaves fall
the sky turn rooftop grey.

The dog chases alongside the bike, barking. She leaves it behind.

MUM   Don't ride into the wind Evelyn. It will hurt your
ears.
DAD   It's going to snow.
MUM   Cover your ears. *(Dad covers his ears)* Not you, you
silly man – Evelyn.
EVELYN   Look Mum – no hands.
MUM   Be careful.
DAD   She's testing herself.
MUM   She's testing me.
EVELYN   Cheerio.

New section: the scene now fully winter – she peddles on.

EVELYN   The sky
loses shape
when it's about to snow.
The wind drops
to the ground
and lies still.
All the fields
look strange
unknown
Hidden by snow
that sinks me
up to the knee
All around me

a white muffler
all sound smothered.

I listen
but my ears
tell me nothing.
There is no sound,
no sound
no sound...

The world
has lost its voice.
It cannot reach me. *(pause)*
I'm lost.

MUM   I told her not to go.

DAD   I'll find her.

EVELYN   The snow defeats the wheels.
I push the bike forward
Into the white world.

DAD   Evelyn.

EVELYN   Into the silence.

Sound of heart beat. Movement section: her father searches for her, calls out her name, at first loudly but gradually descending into silence. She pushes on into the silence. Suddenly he finds her.

DAD   Evelyn!

EVELYN   Dad!

DAD   I've been calling your name over and over.

EVELYN   What?

DAD   Are you alright?

EVELYN   My ears hurt... it's all so quiet... and everywhere looks the same.

DAD   Long as you're alright... leave the bike here, I'll give you a lift home.

She climbs on his back. He begins to walk.

EVELYN   Dad?

DAD   What now?

EVELYN   Can you hear me thinking?

DAD   No. What were you thinking?

EVELYN   I was thinking – *(sound of piano)* I was thinking... I would be a musician – a real one.

DAD *(out of breath)* And what would you play?

EVELYN   I'm good at the piano...

DAD   Aye – you are.

EVELYN   Shall I tell you a secret?

DAD   If you want –

EVELYN   Sometimes, when I play the piano – *(Sound of piano: very gentle.)* ...I close my eyes and forget who I am... and when I stop playing... the music just carries on... inside me, like I was a bell ringing all by myself.

The scene becomes abstract as he lifts Evelyn. The movement expresses their deep connection and his total support of her. The piano fades and he is walking through the snow.

EVELYN   On my father's back,
               lifted through the world,
               a child returns home
               out of the snow
               safe and sound.

               On my father's back
               I ride... and listen
               to his breathing
               listen to the beating
               of his heart.
               On my father's back
               I ride...

COLIN   Is she alright?

ROGER	Is she going to live?
MUM	Out! Out!
DAD	Ssh now… she's sleeping.
COLIN	Pretending to.
DAD	Go and feed the pigs – the both of you.

The boys exit.

MUM	Testing herself, I suppose?
DAD	She's a very determined lass. It'll come in use one day…
MUM	Determined? Stubborn more like.
DAD	Sometimes you have to be stubborn, to get where you want in life.
MUM	I'm worried for her.
DAD	For why?
MUM	She keeps saying that her ears hurt.
DAD	I'm sure it's nothing to worry about.
MUM	It seems worse than before and sometimes she doesn't seem to hear me at all. *(Silence)* She says she loves music – wants to be a concert pianist.
DAD	Aye told me the same–
MUM	Perhaps we should get her ears tested.
DAD	Aye, no harm in that… don't worry now.
MUM	You worry too… only you hide it.
DAD	After Christmas then – a test.

Evelyn is still asleep. The scene changes around her. Music. The transition is dream like but the scene that follows is real. She wakes into reality, as if out of the dream of childhood. She sits on a chair in a spotlight. Enter a woman in a white coat.

WOMAN	I understand you like tests. *(Evelyn nods)* We test everyone… you're no one special. *(Evelyn shakes her head)*

It's a hearing test... These are headphones...
Do you like headphones? *(Evelyn nods)*
Some children don't like headphones.
(Evelyn is unsure whether to shake or nod. She puts on a pair of headphones. As she does so the woman wheels a desk in front of her. On the desk is what looks like a board game with counters on.)
This is very simple... When you hear a little bleep, I want you to move the counter to another space. You understand?
(Evelyn nods. A quiet bleep. Evelyn sits impassive. Repeat. The bleep gets louder but still Evelyn does not hear.)
You're not trying very hard. Listen to the bleeps.

EVELYN   What? *(She lifts headphones)*

WOMAN *(annoyed)* Listen to the bleeps.

We hear a loud bleep.

WOMAN   Why didn't you move the counter? Come on now try harder. *(Another bleep, really quite loud. Still Evelyn does not hear.)* You're being very difficult

Another bleep. The woman writes the results on a piece of paper.

WOMAN   I thought you liked tests.

This paper is now given to a doctor [male]. Evelyn remains seated through this mini transition in which her parents enter as if waiting outside the consultation room. Evelyn hums to herself. A clock ticks. Mum waits outside, tapping her feet. Dad is outside the building, reading the paper, whistling. All these sound louder than reality. When the doctor turns to Evelyn they both stop as if they can hear what's going on in the room.

DOCTOR   Evelyn... these are the results of several hearing tests, which indicate that your hearing has got worse. Is that true? *(She nods)* Are you having problems in school? *(She shakes her head)* Hearing the teachers? *(She nods)* Can you hear me now?

(She nods and he turns away)
Can you hear me now? *(Silence)*
Can you hear me Evelyn? *(He turns back)*
Can you hear me now?

EVELYN   Yes. Of course.

DOCTOR   You're lip reading? That's useful, but it must be hard at school if the teacher is facing the blackboard. You'll have to tell the teacher you need her to face the front, otherwise you'll not know what's being said and you'll fall behind in your work. Are you falling behind in your work, Evelyn?

EVELYN   ... Yes.

DOCTOR   So what can you hear... say, in the playground?

EVELYN   I hate the playground. I stay in and practise the piano.

DOCTOR   But what does the playground sound like?

We hear this noise as if in her head.

EVELYN   Like mashed potato.

DOCTOR   I see... Now just try this wee hearing aid for me and we'll see if we can turn the mashed potato into something – more edible. *(He fixes the aid)* You like music I'm told?

EVELYN   I love music. I'm going to be a musician.

DOCTOR   I see... Well with this little contraption you should be able to hear yourself play the piano quite clearly. It will take a little getting used to... twiddle with the volume and with a bit of luck you'll hear things you haven't heard for ages. What do you hear now?

EVELYN   I hear...

We hear what she hears – the street outside, voices, cars, snatches of music, a sound-scape develops under which is gradually heard the heart beat sound which underpins the following scene. Again the scene changes round Evelyn but the 'test' chair remains.

EVELYN   Whole seasons passed,
Xmas trees came and went.

Test followed test
Every summer we pitched the tent
Every autumn we took it down.
Test followed test...
Whole seasons passed.
It's August now... time...

Time to follow my brothers
up to the big school.

COLIN	It's no problem.
ROGER	We'll look after you.
EVELYN	I don't need looking after.
MUM	Are you ready Evelyn? Evelyn...?
ROGER	Mum's calling, can't you hear?
COLIN	Turn up the hearing aid –
EVELYN	It is turned up.
ROGER	Perhaps the batteries are flat?
EVELYN	They're new.

The brothers look at each other.

EVELYN	What?
COLIN	Nothing.
MUM	Come on Evelyn. We'll be late.
EVELYN	It's not time for school yet.
MUM	No – no you have another hearing test.
COLIN	Another one?
EVELYN	It's only a test.
DAD	That's the spirit.

Heart beat sound continues as parents take up previous positions.
The same doctor enters. Silence. She sits in the chair.

DOCTOR	So – how's the lip reading?
EVELYN	I don't really think about it.

DOCTOR   Mmm... and how does the playground sound these days?

EVELYN   It sounds like...

We hear a mish mash of sound but very faint this time.

DOCTOR   Like mashed potato. Even with the hearing aids?

EVELYN   Yes.

He ushers in Evelyn's mother.

MUM   Is everything alright?

DOCTOR   I'm afraid – we're going to have to be realistic...

MUM   What do you mean – realistic?

DOCTOR   Evelyn has suffered a gradual loss of hearing – *(pause)* you're going to have to send her to a special school, for the deaf.

MUM   She's not deaf –

EVELYN   What did he say?

Heartbeat gets louder.

EVELYN   I watch them talking.
I watch their lips moving
My mother's face is pale
with shock and worry.

DOCTOR   I assure you it's a very good school.

MUM   But she's set her heart on the same school as her brothers.

EVELYN   Outside Dad is leaning on the car... He doesn't know that *I'm deaf.*

DOCTOR   She's probably been able to hide her deafness and find ways of coping.

MUM   But how did it happen?

DOCTOR   Some gradual damage to the nerves... Why, I don't know – we may never know – but I do know that Evelyn is profoundly deaf.

EVELYN   I feel strange – different.
The world is changing shape in front of me.
It shifts and sighs
becoming flat and white,
and something tells me,
that when I leave this room
nothing will be quite the same again.

I will be deaf – it's official – and silence
falls around me like snow.

DAD *(steps forward)* What is it? What's the matter?

MUM   I had no idea...

DAD   You're shaking...

MUM   The doctor says Evelyn's profoundly deaf. He says she has to go to a school for the deaf... in Aberdeen.

EVELYN   I don't want to go. I'm not going. I'm not going.

DAD   Don't shout Evelyn.

EVELYN   I'm not shouting.

DAD   Yes you are. You just can't hear yourself.

EVELYN   I want to go to the same school as my friends.

MUM   But the doctor was quite clear –

EVELYN   I'm not going. I'm not deaf.

DAD   Well... there's no need I suppose to hang on the doctor's coat tails...

MUM   But he said –

DAD   We can go at a steady pace here – not rush around.

MUM   Perhaps we should have rushed around a little sooner and this may not have happened. *(Silence)* She won't be able to cope.

DAD   We don't know that. Besides, her brothers will help her.

EVELYN   I don't need help.

DAD   We all need help Evelyn. I mean – could I run the farm without your mother?

MUM   Hush now... I'm the one that runs the farm... with your help.

DAD   Exactly. So... try the big school on for size. And if it doesn't fit, we'll think again.

EVELYN   Mum...?

Evelyn's Mum smiles bravely and nods in agreement.

DAD   A big school it is too.

Roger rings the school bell, triggering a movement / sound piece conjuring up the transition to the big school. The others dress Evelyn in her new uniform. This dressing and the way it's done can be a recurring pattern in the story – expressing the whole notion of patterns in life and music, form and content.

EVELYN   I like the big school
but I don't tell anyone that I'm deaf.
Why should I? I'm the same as everyone else.
I can cope.

TEACHER   Evelyn?

EVELYN   Yes, sir.

TEACHER   Wait for me outside the percussion room. *(exit)*

EVELYN   Yes sir. *(Aside)* The percussion room.

Silence. Then sound of heart beat. She steps inside the room – a magical sound fills the air. This is an 'Aladdin's Cave' for Evelyn. The stage begins to fill with percussion instruments, which from now on will gradually fill the performing space, as music becomes more central to her life. She moves among the instruments and plays each in turn. The teacher enters just after she's hit the tam tam. The Teacher has a piece of paper in his hand.

TEACHER   Do you know what a paradox is?

EVELYN   Is it a bird?

TEACHER   No...
It says here you have no musical ability – cannot tell a high note
from a low note but it also says here you have passed six grades
on the piano – that's a paradox. Is there something you should tell
me?

EVELYN   No sir. I don't think so, sir.

TEACHER   But Evelyn according to this test –
you have no musical ability, at all.
You have no sense of pitch.
You have no sense of tone.
Perhaps music is not the right thing for you.

EVELYN   I love music. I'm going to be a musician in the
orchestra .

TEACHER   The piano may not be –

EVELYN   That's why I was thinking about... the drums.

TEACHER   Percussion? Do you know what percussion is?

Evelyn is puzzled by the question.

EVELYN   Rhythm?

TEACHER   Aye – but its more... Do you ever lose your temper
Evelyn? *(She nods)* And what do you feel like doing when you
lose your temper?

EVELYN   I feel like...

TEACHER   Like striking out? *(She nods)* But you know that's
wrong, so you strike a drum instead. In other words – it's about
feelings – emotions, but not just anger; excitement, fear,
happiness – you have to... to... hit from the heart. *(He shows her
the instruments, hitting each as he goes.)* This is a vibraphone...
this is a Marimba and these are drums... a Timpani and that thing
you were whacking so energetically just now... is a Tam Tam...
and that I take it is a hearing aid? Why didn't you tell us?

EVELYN   I can cope. If I watch people's lips, I can tell what
they're saying most of the time. I want to be in the school
orchestra.

TEACHER   But if you can't hear the sounds?

EVELYN   I *can* hear. Not *hear* exactly... I *sort* of hear it.

TEACHER   What kind of *sort* of?

EVELYN   Inside me... the sound...goes right through me.

TEACHER   In a moment I'm going to make two different sounds and I want you to tell me what they are... but first, close your eyes... go on.

He slams a door then clashes a cymbal.

EVELYN   A door shutting... a cymbal crashing.

TEACHER   That's remarkable... it's –

EVELYN   A paradox?

TEACHER   Aye – Wait... *(excited now)*... put you hands on the wall and close your eyes... I'm going to strike the Timpani and you tell me which note is higher.

He hits the drum.

EVELYN   The second note was higher... I could feel it.

TEACHER   You can feel the difference – between a high note and a low note?

EVELYN   Yes.

TEACHER   Sing... um... 'You take the high road and I'll –'

EVELYN   *(sings out of tune)*... take the low road and I'll be in Scotland afore you...'

TEACHER   But you can't sing in tune.

EVELYN   Inside my head I can sing in tune... inside my head it sounds... perfect.

TEACHER   But the orchestra is outside your head. The orchestra is a whole bunch of sounds – outside of you. You'd have to learn how to distinguish one sound from another. It would be hard, hard work.

EVELYN   I'm a hard worker–

TEACHER   You'll have to learn to count notes like a demon.

EVELYN   I can be a demon – you ask my brothers. I can do it. I can, I can, I can.

TEACHER   Then we'd best be making a start.

Evelyn starts to hit things. He joins in and it develops into the school Orchestra and she is part of it. The following text comes out of and is part of the music.

EVELYN   Learning how to play
              learning how to count
              learning how to listen
              when I cannot hear.
              School life – home life
              falling silent.
              Learning how to play
              day after day
              Learning how to count
              time away.
              School life – home life
              learning how to listen
              when I cannot hear.

Spotlight on Evelyn –Wind. She climbs the grain tower.

EVELYN   Every day the world became a little quieter –
              and the quieter it became
              the more I felt… its rhythm
              in my feet – in my hands
              my legs, my heart…
              my heart…
              And the more I knew
              That music was going to be my life. [*]

---

[*] Possible interval here. Repeat above speech to begin after interval.

Below, her brothers enter, now slightly older. She waves. They wave back, josh each other and then go off in different directions.

EVELYN　　　　Colin...Roger...?
　　　　　　　　Once upon a farm
　　　　　　　　I had two brothers
　　　　　　　　and we fought and fought
　　　　　　　　until one day we
　　　　　　　　ran out of battles.
　　　　　　　　Their lives and mine
　　　　　　　　took different paths.

She climbs down. Dad enters.

EVELYN　　　　Colin... Roger...? Where are they?

DAD　　　　　Playing football or something – I don't know – I never know these days...

EVELYN　　　　What's the matter? What?

DAD　　　　　I had to make a decision Evelyn – about the dog, about Floss... she was getting old – and sick – it didn't seem fair to let her suffer.

EVELYN　　　　You killed her?

DAD　　　　　No, no. I... took her to the vet. I got good advice. We discussed this Evelyn... you remember? So I – I let her go....

EVELYN　　　　What?

DAD　　　　　Come with me... I buried her out here Evelyn. Just here... She had a grand life here with us, didn't she?

EVELYN　　　　Yes.

DAD　　　　　She was getting so old that it was sad to see her struggle so.

EVELYN　　　　Why didn't you let us say goodbye?

DAD　　　　　You'd have persuaded me to do the wrong thing.

EVELYN　　　　It seems so strange – not to see her – ever again.

DAD　　　　　Aye... but you have to think of her... she's better off... out of pain.

EVELYN　　　　I wish people – animals – could live forever.

DAD   Aye... but... you know – *(She looks up at him)*
There comes time... when you're ready... to go... It's just... the
way of things. Nothing stays the same – everything moves on.

EVELYN   I wish it wouldn't.

DAD   It's just now you feel that,
but you'll grow up too – move on – move away.
Then you have to learn to get by on your own.
Everyone has to in the end.

EVELYN   Poor Floss.

DAD   Aye – we'll miss her. But we'll always remember.
And in that way... *(sighs)* ...Sometimes Evelyn there are no
words.

*He exits. Evelyn walks. Music in Evelyn's head. Notes fall like rain
around her – she runs. We hear what is in her head. Enter teacher.*

EVELYN   I've written some music.
I went for a walk
I walked for miles,
and the music
came into my head.
It was just in there...
like sweets in a box.

*She gives this music to her teacher. Enter others in school orchestra,
who mime their instruments and imitate the sounds vocally.*

TEACHER   Okay, let's try it one more time... remember
recorders, you've got Evelyn's tune for the first eight bars...
accordion – you take over at bar nine and Evelyn remember... not
too loud, watch me.

*The school orchestra plays the tune. The others get fed up because
Evelyn plays too loudly sometimes or miscounts. Evelyn's frustration
builds – suddenly the others stop and we only hear her contribution.
The Orchestra disperses in disgust.*

TEACHER   I told you it would be hard work.

EVELYN   Hard work for me. What's wrong with them?

TEACHER   Hard work for them too. Sometimes you play too loud. Sometimes too soft.

Transition through next text to farm.

EVELYN   Whole seasons passed.
Christmas trees came and went
and sometimes I would play too loud,
sometimes I would play too soft.
Sometimes the others would be annoyed with me.
Sometimes I felt like – like –
Sometimes there are no words.

Home. Her father is reading the paper.

DAD   What's the matter Evelyn?

EVELYN   Nothing.

DAD   You're angry about something.

EVELYN   No I'm not.

DAD   Frustrated then.

EVELYN   I'm not frustrated. I can cope.

MUM   What's the matter Evelyn?

EVELYN   Stop asking me that.

MUM   I only asked the once.

DAD   She's fine. She's not frustrated or angry, she is totally without emotion as you can see.

MUM   She has to cheer up. I can't have you moping about the farm like that – you'll worry the animals.

EVELYN *(screams)* You'd mope around, wouldn't you? If you were struggling to hear all day?

Silence.

DAD   You show some respect for your mother! You hear –
(He stops) Some respect.

He goes away.

MUM   Tell me.
EVELYN   Sometimes... I wish, with every beat of my heart
that I could hear what everyone else hears.
I'm not complaining... I'm not, but I can't help wishing it.
Just to hear... simple sounds... water running from a tap,
from a stream, falling on the roof in a storm,
people laughing, clapping, pop songs – anything.
I wish that I could hear your voice. Dad's voice.
MUM   Of course you do.

Evelyn goes and sits outside.

DAD   It's getting dark Evelyn. *(She does not hear.)*
MUM   If I'd kept her indoors, stopped her swimming.
DAD   Impossible –
MUM   Stopped her riding her bike in the cold.
DAD   It's not your fault. No one's fault. It's just one of
those things.

Father gets torch and goes and sits with Evelyn.

EVELYN   Sorry.
DAD   Ach... I could say I understand, but it wouldn't be
the truth.

She shines the torch on his face so that she can lip read.

DAD No one else who can hear, really knows what it's like.
Nobody really knows what it's like to be someone else. *(pause)*
How's school?
EVELYN   Smelly...

DAD   Smelly?

EVELYN   There are two boys in the orchestra who play football all lunch hour and they sweat buckets and then they come into practice... and they stink like stink bombs And they are going to stink all through our marathon.

DAD   What marathon?

EVELYN   I told you about the marathon...

DAD   You're going to run a marathon?

EVELYN   No. Mum's right. You don't listen. It's a music marathon. The newspapers are coming – it's a big thing.

DAD   Well... I forgot – the farm – the pigs –

EVELYN   We play music for eight hours non-stop... to raise money to buy hearing aids and those bucket boys are going to really smell at the end of it.

DAD   I thought you liked the Orchestra?

EVELYN   I might as well not be there. No one can hear a note I play.

DAD   But that's the whole point – it's a group sound. You're part of the group.

EVELYN   I feel lost in the group. It's like being a – a glass of water poured into a bath. You just become part of the whole thing.

DAD   But that's the –

EVELYN   I know that's the point of an orchestra... I'm just...

DAD   If you feel like that you might as well go solo.

EVELYN *(excited)* That's it! That's what I really enjoy – the moment I do the solo and everyone knows that the sounds are my responsibility. I made them and if I get them wrong, it's my fault. That's when I feel – alive.

MUM   What are you talking about?

EVELYN   I'm going to be a solo percussionist.

MUM   Solo?

EVELYN   Why not?

MUM   On your own?

They look at her.

MUM   I mean… there are no parts for solo percussionists,
  are there?

DAD   Are there?

EVELYN   I'll write them myself.

DAD   She'll write them herself.

EVELYN   I'll write one for the marathon.

A concise musical/movement section which represents the money-raising marathon and as it continues she is left playing solo. She gets more and more exhausted. Enter two reporters, one a photographer.

REPORTER   How much money have you raised today Miss
  Glennie?

EVELYN   Three hundred pounds.

PHOTOGRAPHER   Smile?

REPORTER   Is it true… that when you first came to school you
  didn't tell them you were deaf?

EVELYN   Yes.

REPORTER   Why was that?

EVELYN   I had hearing aids. But I don't use them now.

PHOTOGRAPHER   She probably wanted to be like everyone
  else… isn't that right?

REPORTER   And you taught yourself to lip read?

EVELYN   Yes.

REPORTER   How did you do that?

EVELYN   By reading people's lips.

PHOTOGRAPHER   Ha!

REPORTER   When did your hearing first start to deteriorate?

EVELYN   When I was about eight.

REPORTER   How old are you now?

EVELYN   Sixteen. Did you enjoy the music we played? I wrote
  some of it myself.

REPORTER   Talking to you, you'd never know you were deaf…

PHOTOGRAPHER   The music was great.

REPORTER   No. I'm serious... how do you play music so well, being... so... deaf?

PHOTOGRAPHER   She wants to talk about her music.

REPORTER   But that's not the story.

EVELYN   I feel the notes inside me. It depends how hard I hit the drum... it's about pressure... different vibrations mean different things. It's like – having ears on the inside.

REPORTER   Inside ears?

PHOTOGRAPHER   Smile.

REPORTER   You don't have to smile if you don't want to.

PHOTOGRAPHER   Ta.

REPORTER   And what do you want to do when you leave school?

EVELYN   I'm going to be a professional musician. *(They look at each other)* Of course I'll have to go to music college first.

REPORTER   I think you're amazing. We both do.

They turn away.

PHOTOGRAPHER   She's a very talented musician.

REPORTER   For someone who's deaf.

EDITOR *(enters)* Okay – what have you got?

REPORTER   A deaf girl – raising money for the deaf.

PHOTOGRAPHER   She played music for eight hours.

EDITOR   What kind of music?

REPORTER   Percussion.

EDITOR   Is that music?

REPORTER/PHOTOGRAPHER   What do you mean?

EDITOR   Percussion...? It's not music. It's the beat behind the music.

PHOTOGRAPHER   Of course it's music –

REPORTER   It's not just one note – bang bang bang.

PHOTOGRAPHER   It goes up and down – bang

REPORTER   Bang.

PHOTOGRAPHER   Bang.

EDITOR   Is this her? Why's she smiling? She's exhausted, it says, and there she is grinning like a cat.

REPORTER   Told you.

EDITOR   Shut up!

PHOTOGRAPHER   She plays drums, xylophone, timp –

REPORTER   She's got ears on the inside.

PHOTOGRAPHER   She wants to be a professional musician.

REPORTER   Aye, that's the hard part.

EDITOR   Why is that the hard part?

REPORTER   Because it's wrong to give her false hope.

PHOTOGRAPHER   It's wrong to give her no hope at all.

REPORTER   Someone should tell her, 'Child you are deaf. You cannot go to Music College.'

PHOTOGRAPHER   Oh that's your job is it?

EDITOR   Shut up the both of you! *(Studies photo)* I may not know much about music... not as much as you bright sparks, but I do know there's something about this girl.
I like this girl – because I like honest endeavour. I can see it. I can smell it. I've got a nose on the inside when it comes to stories.
So... you and you – follow this girl's story. If she fails – it's sad – we can sell sad. If she succeeds – it's happy. We can sell happy...
Now give me your headline, however bad it may be.

REPORTER   Okay, here goes.

REPORTER/PHOTOGRAPHER *(sing)*
            She's got style
            She's got grace
            She's got flare

            She's got taste
(in close harmony) But wouldn't you know ?–

EDITOR   No.

The photographer stands back and lets the reporter sing alone.

REPORTER *(sings)* She's as deaf as a stone.

EDITOR   That's the headline? Deaf as a stone?

REPORTER   What's wrong with that?

EDITOR   You can't say that…

REPORTER Why not?

EDITOR   Because it's crude, it's rude, it's coarse, it's cheap and it probably isn't even true.

PHOTOGRAPHER Told you.

REPORTER Why don't you think of a headline, Editor, sir?

EDITOR   Shut up! I'll think of a headline. *(Drum roll)* Amazing Evelyn – Deaf but she makes music!
(Silence) Shall I say it again?

PHOTOGRAPHER No, no. It's perfect – precise – clever.

REPORTER   And it has a kind of anti-rhythm all of its own.

EDITOR *(very annoyed)* Print the story and the photo – and my headline! Do it!

The Reporter and the Photographer repeat the headline over and over until they find a funky tune to go with it. In music and movement the newspaper is printed and lands in Dad's lap.

DAD   'Amazing Evelyn – Deaf, but she makes music.' The press seem to be taking an interest in Evelyn.

MUM   There's no harm in a bit of publicity.

EVELYN   No. Now the whole world knows I'm deaf.

DAD   I don't think they read 'The People's Aberdeen Journal' all over the world.

EVELYN   But why do they say 'Evelyn, the deaf musician'? They don't say 'Paul McCartney, the hearing guitarist' do they?

DAD   Who's Paul McCartney?

He exits.

MUM   He's teasing.

EVELYN   Why?

MUM   You mustn't take yourself too seriously Evelyn – that's all.

EVELYN   I want to be a professional musician. It's serious to me.

MUM   Yes, Evelyn – we know. We know.

Evelyn's mother gives her a hug. Music. Around Daughter and Mother image there is a transition into Careers Office, which is not a realistic set up but reflects Evelyn's emotional state.

CAREERS OFFICER *(shouts)* So you know why we're here?
EVELYN   To talk about my career.
C.OFFICER *(shouts)* We're here to talk about your Career –
EVELYN   I can't hear so you don't have to shout.
C.OFFICER   You lip read?
EVELYN   I'm getting better at it.
C.OFFICER   No hearing aid?
EVELYN   No.
C.OFFICER   So – what kind of job do you want to do?
EVELYN   I'm going to be a professional musician.

The Careers Officer smiles.

EVELYN *(aside)* I hate that smile.
C.OFFICER   A professional musician?
EVELYN   I'll need to go to a music college.
C.OFFICER   You're a bright girl. You have several O' levels.
EVELYN *(aside)* She hasn't heard me.
C.OFFICER   Why not try Law?
EVELYN *(aside)* She's deaf on the outside.
C.OFFICER   You could help other disabled people?
EVELYN   I'm not disabled.
C.OFFICER   Let's start again.
EVELYN   I told you I want to be a musician. I'm going to play in London with the schools percussion ensemble.
C.OFFICER *(sharply)* Evelyn! *(silence)* You can be a musician... and a wonderful – hobby, it will be... but it can't be a job. Not for you.
EVELYN   I know what I want. I'm very determined.

C.OFFICER   You force me to be honest. Evelyn...you are deaf.

EVELYN *(aside)* I could scream.

Wind sound begins.

C.OFFICER   Deaf people do not become professional musicians. And don't tell me about Beethoven... Beethoven was a genius. It's impossible for you. It's better to accept it now and avoid disappointment later on. You must give this idea up. However much you enjoy music. There are other things you can do.

Wind blows. She stands on the chair and is now at the top of the grain tower.

C.OFFICER   Why not be a teacher, a hairdresser, a nanny, an accountant?

EVELYN *(screams, then hits several instruments very hard)*

Exit Careers Officer. Enter Father with letter.

DAD   Evelyn! *(He exits)*

EVELYN   Now that I'm bigger
                 the view from the top of the grain tower
                 is smaller.
                 I can no longer hear the wind
                 though I feel it my hair.
                 I feel...

DAD *(enters)* Evelyn! Evelyn!

She climbs down.

DAD   Your music teacher wrote to a woman called um... Mrs Rachlin... a lovely letter she wrote too... um she wrote to a Mrs Rachlin ... yes I said that... and they run something called 'The Beethoven Fund for deaf children.' Are you getting this?

EVELYN   Yes.

DAD   They want to see you and if they think that it's possible for you to become a professional musician they will help you apply to the Royal Academy of Music in London. That's in London. The Royal Academy...

She hugs him.

DAD   But – you have to do another test.

Sound of heart beat. Enter Mrs Rachlin and the Doctor. Evelyn is back in the test chair. The Doctor places some plastic cups in front of her.

DOCTOR   Now Evelyn... Mrs Rachlin here, tells me you are an exceptionally talented musician. I believe her. That is no longer in question. The question now is – is it possible for you to study – at a music college, keep up with the other students and eventually become a professional musician in an orchestra? That's what Mrs Rachlin needs to know– to support your application to the Royal Academy of Music. I have therefore been asked to give you a hearing test to see if this is possible.

EVELYN   I understand.

DOCTOR   It's a very simple test. All you have to do is acknowledge me whenever you hear me beat the drum.

EVELYN   A simple test. *(Drum)*
An all important test. *(Drum)*
A test I can't afford
to fail. *(Drum)*
I begin to sweat.
The drum feels so far away...
So far away...

Sound of wind.

EVELYN   I can't do this test
my thoughts drift...

The snowscape returns.

EVELYN   I remember long ago
pushing my bike into the silence,
into the snow.
All around me
a white muffler,
all sound smothered.
I listen
but my ears tell me nothing.
And then...

FATHER'S VOICE   Evelyn.

EVELYN   My father's voice.

FATHER'S VOICE   No one else, who can hear, really knows. No one really knows what it's like to be someone else.

Back to the reality of the test.

EVELYN   A simple test?
An all important test
that I'm failing... because...?
Because this is not the right test. *(pause)*
Mrs Rachlin?

MRS RACHLIN Evelyn, I've spoken to the doctor .It's not good news I'm afraid. I know how important music is to you but if you can't hear, you can't learn. You won't be able to manage and you will never get a job in an orchestra. That's his opinion and it's mine too. I'm sorry. Please don't be upset.

EVELYN   I'm not upset, Mrs Rachlin. All I ask is that you come to the Albert Hall in London and watch me play. I'll show you. Will you come?

MRS RACHLIN Of course...

Transition. Evelyn puts on the concert dress as at start of play. Sound of an orchestra / ensemble, tuning up. A single pure note.

EVELYN   This is it.
The moment.
All my life I've worked
for this moment.
They say I will never be a musician.
Today I will prove them wrong.
All the long hours of practise
slip into this moment
and I revel in it
and hear in my head
and in my heart
every single note.

The Baton falls. The orchestra plays. The whole cast and solo for Evelyn. The music here is intense and formal rather than climactic. We see Evelyn's sticks surreally waving in the air, a flurry of movement. Music ends. Sound of heartbeat remains. Flowers descend as if by magic. Mrs Rachlin steps forward.

EVELYN   Well…? Will you help me? What did you think?

MRS RACHLIN What can I say? I was wrong about you. As soon as you lifted the sticks I knew. You looked so right!

Evelyn does not know what to say so she thrusts the flowers into Mrs Rachlin's arms.

MRS RACHLIN I'll do everything I can to help you Evelyn. Now, all we have to do is to persuade the Royal Academy of Music to give you an audition. They won't believe a deaf girl can achieve what you have achieved, so you'll have to show them, like you've shown me.

EVELYN   Another test?

MRS RACHLIN Then… after the audition comes the hard part. You go home and wait for the letter.

Sound of heart beat. Evelyn climbs the Grain tower in her concert dress. Enter the Reporter and Photographer with Editor.

EDITOR　　　So how's our deaf drummer?

PHOTOGRAPHER　　She played at the Royal Albert Hall.

EDITOR　　　Headline? Go on.

REPORTER *(sings)* 'Plucky deaf girl'

PHOTOGRAPHER *(sings)* 'Musical talent triumphs over deafness'

REPORTER *(sings)* 'Deaf girl tunes into the sound of music'

EDITOR　　　Better, that's better.

PHOTOGRAPHER　　That's better?

EDITOR　　　What now?

PHOTOGRAPHER　　Now she's auditioned for the Royal Academy of Music!

EDITOR　　　That's my girl. Will she get in? *(silence)* Well?

REPORTER　　She doesn't stand a hope in hell.

EDITOR　　　You?

PHOTOGRAPHER　　She's got guts. Never takes no for an answer.

REPORTER　　The girl's deaf! How can a deaf person become a professional musician? There's no way and he knows it. We all know it.

EDITOR　　　So the story ends in tears? *(sighs)* Ah well...we can sell that.

Transition back to farm.

EVELYN　　　When I was a child, I lived on a farm.
I climbed the grain tower.
It was ever so high
tall as a tower in a fairy story.
When I was a child
we had a dog called Floss
she died and my father buried her
over there – behind the Hen house.

And there's the pale patch of grass
where my brothers used to pitch the tent in summer
and in the autumn light bonfires.

We fought all year round.

From the top of the grain tower
I can see the whole farm
and beyond the farm, the fields
beyond the fields – the future…

MUM   Evelyn! Evelyn!

DAD   She's up the grain tower – again.

EVELYN   Hello!

MUM   Come down! Come down! There's a letter from London. *(She comes down)* From the Royal Academy of Music. It says so… there.

DAD   Well, open it.

EVELYN   'Dear Evelyn… following your recent audition, we are pleased to offer you a place at the Royal Academy of Music. Congratulations. Term starts on September 3rd.'

DAD   Yes!   *(He cannot contain himself and hops about with excitement.)*

MUM   Now, now… don't get over excited.

DAD   Why? Why not? Why not? *(He pulls them into a jig)*

MUM   Oh Evelyn… you've worked so hard.

DAD   Just wait, till I tell your brothers.

Music. Enter the two brothers at speed. They steal the letter.

COLIN   Ooh! The Royal Academy of Music.

ROGER   An' I thought you were going to be a potato picker.

COLIN   At the Royal Academy of Scullers.

She chases them for the letter.

EVELYN   Aren't you ever going to grow up?

COLIN   Aren't you ever going to learn to take a joke?

ROGER   We're only teasing.

COLIN   Teasing… Tarenzeening.

ROGER   We think it's great…

COLIN   Well, I do cos I have a brain, whereas Roger…

EVELYN   Stop it.

ROGER   Now you sound like Mum.

ROGER/COLIN Stop it! Stop it! Stop it!

COLIN   We'll miss you.

ROGER   On the farm.

COLIN   Present.

He gives her the toy drum she used to bash to annoy them.

EVELYN   I love my brothers.
I hate my brothers.
I love my brothers.

Final transition moment. Enter parents with suitcase for Evelyn. They dress Evelyn in coat and hat for the trip to London.

MUM   London. Why does everything have to be in London?

Enter the Reporter and Photographer.

PHOTOGRAPHER   Congratulations… we knew you could do it.

REPORTER   Never doubted it for a moment. And now you're off to the big city.

PHOTOGRAPHER   To become a professional musician.

REPORTER   A dream come true.

PHOTOGRAPHER *(takes photo)* You don't have to smile if you don't want to.

REPORTER   There's just one last question…

PHOTOGRAPHER   Here he goes…

Music.

REPORTER If you could have one wish in the world would you have your hearing back? If I had your hearing in my hand, would you take it?

EVELYN   No...

PHOTOGRAPHER Told you.

EVELYN   This is me.

REPORTER Me is a very determined person.

Sound of train.

PHOTOGRAPHER   One last photo –

REPORTER *(aside, writes in notebook)* 'Scottish lass on road to musical career?'

As the photo is being taken, the parents step forward. The sound of the train station builds. Announcements of 'Train leaving for London in two minutes...'etc.

MUM   Look after yourself.

DAD   Work hard.

MUM   Enjoy yourself.

DAD   Play from the heart.

MUM   Write.

EVELYN *(aside)* I feel so...

Climactic final music section, in which whole cast through percussion express Evelyn's excitement and achievement.

Lights fade.
The End

Plays produced and published

Plays for young people

The monkey and the crocodile   Theatre Centre
Don't she look funny   York YPT
The Flood   Unicorn Theatre + BBC Radio 5.
Inner City Limits   Gwent Theatre.
Playing from the Heart   Polka Theatre.
Eye of the Storm   Snap Theatre.
Hitting home   Dukes Playhouse, Lancaster.
Witness   Dukes Playhouse, Lancaster.
In Living Memory   Gwent Theatre + Radio Wales.
A spell of cold weather   Theatre Centre + Sherman Theatre.
Looking out to see   Sherman Theatre.
The Search for Odysseus   Made in Wales + Theatre Clwyd.
Red Red Shoes   Unicorn Theatre + The Place

Adaptations

Beauty and the Beast   Library Theatre, Manchester.
Cinderella   Library Theatre, Manchester.
Sleeping Beauty   Polka Theatre, London.
The Borrowers   Polka Theatre, London.
Alice, an adventure in Wonderland Unicorn Theatre + Regents Park
                                        Open Air Theatre.

Other Plays

Dead Man's Hat   Orchard Theatre.
Fall of the Roman Empire   Hijinx Theatre.
In the Bleak Midwinter   Hijinx theatre.
Paradise Drive   Hijinx Theatre.
Ill Met by Moonlight   Hijinx Theatre.
Somebody Loves You   New Perspectives Theatre Co.
She Scored for Wales   Gwent Theatre.
Funny Boys   Gwent Theatre + BBC Radio 4
The Stone Throwers   Spectacle Theatre.
Oh Journeyman   Made in Wales Stage Company.
The Dove Maiden   Hijinx Theatre.

Large-scale Community Plays

Bordertown   for Monmouth.
A Song of Streets   Opera for Cardiff [W.N.O]
The Mystery Cycle   for Exmouth.
One Giant Leap   Diversions Dance, Cardiff

Adaptations

Lorna Doone   Orchard Theatre.
Humbug   Gwent Theatre.
On the Black Hill   Made In Wales Stage Co. + BBC Radio 4
Frankenstein   Orchard Theatre.
Sweeney Todd   Orchard Theatre.
Ash on a young man's sleeve   Sherman Theatre.
Independent people   New Perspectives Theatre Co.
The Nativity   Theatr Clwyd.

Other works for TV and Radio include

Trade Winds   BBC Radio Wales.
A Journey in Hell   BBC Radio Wales.
No Borders   A film poem BBC 2 Wales.
The Gate   A play for voices, Radio Wales.
Swallows and Amazons   (adaptation) BBC Radio 4
Telling the sea   (adaptation) BBC Radio 4
A figure of eight   TV play for teenagers *Scene*, BBC2.

Publications

Three Plays,   Seren Books
Looking out to see,   Seren Books [One act plays from Wales]
The Flood,   Collins Educational Books
In The Bleak Midwinter,   Exeter University Press.
The Search for Odysseus,   Aurora Metro Press, in *'Young Blood'*
plays for young performers anthology, edited by Sally Goldsworthy.

Awards and nominations

In the Bleak Midwinter – nominated Best Touring Play, Manchester
Evening News Awards 1992
The Search for Odysseus and *Sleeping Beauty* – nominated for Best
Children's Play, Writers Guild Awards 1994 and 1995.
A Spell of Cold Weather – Winner of Best Children's Play, Writers
Guild awards 1996
No Borders – nominated for BAFTA Cymru 1998
Playing From the Heart – nominated Best Play for young people,
TMA/Equity Awards 1999.